Talking to Fireflies, Shrinking the Moon

Nature Activities for All Ages

Edward Duensing

Fulcrum Publishing
Golden, Colorado

This book is dedicated to
Veronica Duensing and Edward Duensing, Sr.

How wonderful it was to grow up with
a father who could grow the best flowers and
a mother who would never let a glorious sunset pass unappreciated

Text copyright © 1997 Edward Duensing
Originally published by Plume, an imprint of New American Library, a division of Penguin Books USA Inc., © 1990, ISBN 0-452-26511-8

Cover image © 1997 Wayne McLoughlin
Chapter art © 1997 Deborah Rich, except for mountain laurel, originally created by Lois Sloan
Book design by Deborah Rich

Library of Congress Cataloging-in-Publication Data

Duensing, Edward.
      Talking to fireflies, shrinking the moon : nature activities for
  all ages / Edward Duensing.
          p. cm.
  Originally published: New York, N.Y. : Plume, © 1990.
  Includes index.
  ISBN 1-55591-310-5 (pbk.)
      1. Natural history—Outdoor books. 2. Nature study—Activity
  programs. I. Title.
  [QH81.D835   1997]
  508–dc21   96-48840
                                        CIP

Printed in the United States of America
0   9   8   7   6   5   4   3   2

Fulcrum Publishing
350 Indiana Street, Suite 350
Golden, Colorado 80401-5093
(800) 992-2908 · (303) 277-1623

Contents

Acknowledgments

Writing this book has not been an act of assemblage, but a process of discovery that began years ago in a place I have always known as "the woods." There was Split Rock, the Big Swamp, Gaede's Pond, Lava Mountain, and a hundred other places whose names are known only to those who grew up there, playing beneath the trees and riding their bicycles along the old roads. It was a time of long summer days, close friends, and quests for adventures that could be finished before dinner.

I owe much to my mother and father, who encouraged my love of nature, and to my sister, Karen, and brothers, Randy and Brent, who were my first playmates in discovering the outdoors. Later, in the wonderful years between toddlerhood and the tempests of adolescence, came those comrades who would share my youth and thus shape this book: Matt Gervald, Don Uren, Malcolm Munro, and Rob Van Varick—good friends through thick and thin.

Much of what is described in this book will appeal to those people who continue to appreciate life's poetry and spontaneity—people like my wife, Lennie, and my friend Joe Van Putten. To these two go my heartfelt thanks, for they are representative of the many adults who will find joy in the activities described and share them with others.

Each activity has been tested over and over, and I should like to thank my sons, Alex, Ben, and Jed; and my old neighbors, Tim, Ryan, and Matt Dale, for their help in making sure these activities were as fascinating as I thought they would be. I would also like to acknowledge Sy Montgomery, Howard Mansfield, Arlene Pashman, and the librarians at Rutgers University and the Piscataway Public Library. Without their encouragement and assistance, I could not have written this book.

The knowledge that this work will add to children's repertoire of outdoor play has given me great satisfaction, but my goal has been to write a book that will help someone, somewhere, feel a little closer to nature. Robert Frost once wrote about a certain type of person he called a "swinger of birches." I have written this book for those who fit Frost's description.

Edward Duensing
Summer 1996

Introduction

It is not enough to take people out of doors.
We must also teach them to enjoy it.

ERNEST THOMAS SETON

One hundred years ago, there probably wasn't a country boy alive who couldn't hypnotize a bullfrog, or a farm girl who wasn't an expert at weaving a chain of daisies. These simple pleasures were a customary part of childhood in rural areas and were handed down from parent to child (or from big kid to little kid) along the fields and streams of the United States and Canada. Today, these same activities that delighted generations of young people can entertain you and your children and add a new dimension to everyone's outdoor play—the enjoyment that comes from actively participating in the natural world surrounding us.

The activities you are about to discover are the hands-on, gee-whiz type that amuse and amaze and help to create those magic moments that both adult and child will always remember. In addition to being entertaining, the activities are educational, providing firsthand experiences with the inner workings of nature and the interconnectedness of the environment. In many ways, they are experiments that will give life to the facts many of us have learned from books.

Each activity is in some way interactive and will either evoke a response from a plant or animal, alter perceptions, or reveal how something wonderful can be created from the very simplest of materials. There are, however, two prerequisites that can help guarantee success: practice and patience. The reason for practice is obvious: it is a fundamental part of learning any new skill. But patience is the more essential of the two elements and is often the harder one for children to learn. In many of the activities it is important to remember that you are dealing with another living, feeling creature—one that may not be hungry, curious, or in the proper state to respond to your attempts to elicit a reaction. Every one of the activities has been tested, so if you don't succeed the first time, try again. It's well worth the effort.

Although there are many different styles of presentation, I prefer to introduce or accompany an activity with a good story. Children, especially younger ones, are always fascinated by tall tales and romantic fantasies, and it is wonderful to watch their faces light up as you perform one of the activities to prove your story is true. Try weaving a spooky tale around the technique described in "Eyes in the Dark," or use the jewelweed to create a story about enchanted leaves that turn to silver. For older children, I usually practice my presentation before trying out a story, but when I am with the little ones, I often make things up as I go along. With either group, a good story that includes a bit of "nature magic" is always appreciated.

The underlying purpose of this book is to teach people that they are a part of the natural world and that their actions have an influence on the environment. Each activity has been chosen because it is safe, non-destructive, lots of fun, and involves species or elements common throughout large portions of the United States and Canada. The primary focus of the book is on activities that can be performed throughout the year or during the warmer seasons. However, several cooler-season activities have been included for those who want to bundle up and enjoy nature during the late fall, winter, and early spring.

I have enjoyed sharing these activities with children, and it has always been very gratifying to watch them spend an afternoon engaged in one of these projects or to see them show off an activity to their friends. Perhaps my greatest reward came the day I watched my son teaching a friend how to hypnotize a frog. I overheard him say, "I learned how to do it from my dad. He knows lots of neat things." These words epitomize the spirit of this book.

Meetings
with Mammals,
Birds, Frogs, & Fish

The Sonic Duel: Bat Versus Moth

During the long, gray twilight of a peaceful summer evening, about the time children are being called in for the night, an aerial struggle is beginning in the sky above our heads.

We don't usually notice this struggle, but it's a matter of life or death for the hungry bats and the moths they hunt. As always, when the stakes are this high, the action is fast and the contest is well worth watching.

The bat is the master hunter of the night sky, and each night, millions of these winged mammals take to the air, scanning the darkness with the most efficient echolocation system in the animal kingdom. A bat cruising an open area emits about 10 high-pitched chirps per second, creating a wide cone of sound waves in front of itself. When any of these sound waves strike an object, they are bounced back, and the reflected sound is picked up by the bat's ultrasensitive ears, alerting it to the fact that there is something ahead. If the bat interprets the echo as "insect ahead," it immediately takes action, speeding up the number of chirps it emits to around 100 per second. The bat is now locked in on its target. If all goes well, the bat will overtake the insect, catch it in one of its wings, and scoop it into its mouth.

If you want to witness how good a bat's sonar is, throw a pebble a few feet in front of a flying bat. If your aim is good and the bat is hungry, it will wheel about and go into a power dive, following your rock down toward the earth. Usually, the bat will realize it has been fooled long before your decoy nears the ground. But sometimes, they seem to get perilously close to the earth before they pull up.

The person who will try this only once is rare. Bats are so fast and incredibly agile that this activity always demands a repeat performance. However, a word of warning is appropriate here: think about where the rock you are throwing up is going to come down. A bump on the head can take all the fun out of things.

It may seem that nature has stacked the deck against night-flying insects by giving the bat the gift of echolocation. But nature never takes sides, and some insects have developed a set of countermeasures to thwart marauding bats. One method of escape used by several species of moth is to simply pick up the bat's signals before the bat can realize there is anything up ahead. This technique works because a bat can detect a flying moth only up to a distance of 10 to 15 feet away, whereas these moths can hear the bat's high-pitched chirps up to 100 feet away. When the moth picks up a bat's signal, it automatically begins to take evasive action. Some moths perform a rapid series of turns, rolls, and wild gyrations, while others simply fold up their wings and drop to the ground. The goal is to get out of the area the bat is scanning. But whatever the moths do, they must do it quickly, because bats fly much faster than moths. These antibat maneuvers seem to work fairly well, for studies have shown that insects capable of using them have a 40 percent less chance of being captured than those that can't hear a bat approaching.

The moths that respond to high-pitched sounds are easy to identify. After dark, go out to a light or screen that is congested with moths and jingle your keys or shake some coins in your hand. If any bat-detecting moths are there, they will begin flying wildly about or let go of the wall and drop to the ground as if stunned. They do this because certain sounds coming from your keys or coins are the same as those made by bats. You can also try using a wineglass that is half full of liquid. Hold the glass by its stem, moisten your finger, and rub it around the rim of the glass in an even, continuous motion. If done properly, you will generate a high-pitched whine that will cause these moths to begin their bat-avoidance reactions.

Sometimes your noisemaking does nothing at all, and sometimes the response is startling. The response depends on the types of moths present and the frequency of the sounds you generate. Try it out, and if the moths start flying wildly about, explain to your companions what is happening. Everyone will be fascinated.

Animal
Hypnosis

The quest for mastery over the minds of wild beasts is an ancient endeavor that springs from a deep-seated human desire for control over the environment.

Throughout history, myths and legends tell of magical people who commanded animals to do their bidding; and even in today's skeptical world, snake charmers, lion tamers, and alligator wrestlers rarely have trouble drawing a crowd. Yet while most techniques used to control animals are beyond the scope of this book, there is one mysterious activity guaranteed to entertain children and adults alike—animal hypnosis, a method of entrancing a wild creature and rendering it unconscious.

Over 3,000 years ago the Talmud described animal hypnosis and its use on lizards, scorpions, and snakes. Some scholars even believe that the biblical account of staffs changing into snakes may be attributed to a technique still used by present-day Egyptian snake charmers to put cobras into a state of rigid paralysis. Humans have hypnotized iguanas, owls, ducks, chickens, turkeys, swans, guinea pigs, rabbits, mice, crocodiles, crabs, newts, and dozens of other animals, large and small; but the most frequent subject of this activity is the frog.

As with most magic, "bewitching" frogs (to use a phrase from my childhood) is not very difficult once you know the trick. Simply pick up a frog, turn it over, and gently rub your finger up and down its belly. The frog will struggle for a short while but will soon fall into a trance. Continue rubbing for a few more seconds and the trance will become deep enough that the sleeping amphibian can be set down on a smooth surface where it will remain motionless and unaware of its surroundings. The actual process is not very difficult, but if this activity is presented with the sort of sideshow patter that creates an air of anticipation, you can make it blossom into a grand event.

Once the frog has been put into a trance, it will lie immobile with its eyes open, its back legs stretched out, and its forelegs held close to its body. The trance can last anywhere from several minutes to an hour and will not harm the frog in any way. However, you should take care to assure that the frog will not dry out. Amphibians need their bodies moist, and the trance you are inducing can be so powerful that some frogs may not awaken even though they begin to shrivel from lack of moisture and drying effects of the sun. Try to keep your frog out of direct sunlight, and be sure to put it back in water every 10 to 15 minutes, so that no harm will come to it.

While in a trance, the frog will be oblivious to most of the sounds and movements that surround it. You should avoid loud noises, and to keep children from fidgeting while watching the motionless animal, I like to tell them the story of how people in India supposedly once used animal hypnosis to tame wild elephants.

The story takes place in the olden days when elephants were used for heavy work throughout India. First, the people would capture a wild elephant and bind it to a large tree with heavy ropes or chains. The elephant would trumpet and thrash about wildly, straining against its bonds. But once the enraged beast was restrained, the trainers would approach it and begin to slowly wave large, leafy boughs to and fro in front of it. As the trainers waved the boughs, they would sing the same monotonous song over and over, relieving one another as they tired. The process would go on hour after hour until the elephant wearied and began to blink its eyes. The trainers would continue to sing their droning song, and a short while later, the elephant's eyes would shut and its body would relax. This hypnotic process made a wild elephant somewhat docile, and when it awoke the trainers would yoke it to a tame elephant until they could trust it to work alone with a human. If the newly trained elephant relapsed and began to act wild and aggressive, the branch waving and singsong chanting was performed again. Usually it took only a few minutes to bring the elephant back into line.

At the end of the story, if your frog has not awakened by itself and you want to end the demonstration, simply clap your hands or give the animal a light poke with a finger. Either of these actions, or any other abrupt stimulus, will bring the frog back to full consciousness without any period of intermediate grogginess. Frogs can be hypnotized over and over again, so if the children look as if they are ready for a repeat performance, just turn your frog over and begin rubbing its belly again. In a matter of seconds the frog will be back in a trance and unable to move.

Bullfrogs, pickerel frogs, green frogs, leopard frogs, and every other species of frog I have ever caught are susceptible to hypnotism, but toads can sometimes be entirely immune to the procedure. Should children bring you one of these creatures, try to hypnotize it and explain to them that this animal is different from a frog. If the toad doesn't fall into a trance, pick it up, grasping it with one finger on each of its sides, and hold it near the children's ears. Toads held this way often make a squeaky, chirping sound that always gets kids to smile, especially when you tell them what the toad is supposedly saying.

There is considerable disagreement about animal hypnosis in the scientific community. In fact, scientists can't even agree upon a proper name for the phenomenon, which has been labeled as catalepsy, death feigning, akinesis, mesmerism, paroxysmal inhibition, and tonic immobility, just to name a few. But far greater than the difference in names is the variation in theories used to explain this hypnotic phenomenon.

Charles Darwin and others believed that the trance was a defense against predators and helped the animals who used it to survive. Most prey animals freeze in position when they first spot a predator and then flee if the distance between themselves and the predator decreases. If the predator catches its prey, the captured animal will fight to regain its freedom. It is when this struggle is unsuccessful that some animals lapse into a trance. This last strategy may be effective because predators respond to the movements and vocalizations of their prey and cease their attacks once the captured animal lies motionless. One study found that 29 of 50 ducks caught by foxes survived their initial capture and handling by falling into a trance. Some of the ducks were even carried off and cached by the fox for later use, but they awoke after their captors had departed and escaped relatively unharmed.

To some degree, this theory of animal hypnosis explains the fainting behavior opossums display when confronted with danger as well as the paralysis that comes over frogs when their abdomens are stroked. Above all, a demonstration of this hypnotic power illustrates, in a harmless manner, the power human beings can have over the lives of animals. Should we carelessly destroy the lives and habitats of animals just because we have the power to do so? Or should we care for our planet and all the creatures on it? These questions are something everyone should think about, and the sight of an entranced animal stretched out helplessly before you may help you find the answers.

Fish Watching

We normally don't work at spotting fish. We either see them or we don't. But this reliance on serendipity instead of strategy causes us to miss some interesting sights as we walk along a stream or pond.

It is an unfortunate state of affairs, yet by understanding how fish sense the world around them, we can correct the problem and add a new dimension to our walks near the shores of aquatic environments.

The fact that rays of light are refracted, or bent, when they penetrate the surface of water is well known. Everyone learns about this in elementary science classes. But what few people are aware of is the fact that the refraction of light makes the world above the water look very different to a fish. In fact, because of this refraction, fish see things in places where they really aren't.

When a fish looks up, it sees a transparent "hole" in the surface of the water directly overhead. To the sides of this hole nothing above the surface can be seen, but looking through the hole is like looking into a magic window that shows the fish not only what is directly overhead, but also what is off to the sides or on a nearby shore.

Fish see the world above this way because the light that enters the water continues to carry the same images even though it is bent downward. This refraction gives the fish a periscopic view of the world above. Not only can a fish see what is directly overhead, at 90 degrees above its position; it can also see everything down to 20 degrees above the surface of the water.

Many successful anglers realize that because of the refraction of light, a fish near the shore will see them before they can see it. Watch them. Notice how some may actually crouch down as they near the water, always staying below a 20-degree angle with the water's surface. They know that if a big fish sees them coming, they might as well save their bait. That fish will be gone before they even get to the shore.

You can experience this fish-eye view of the world any time you are swimming. Go out to where the water is about three or four feet deep and look around for prominent landmarks on the shore—lifeguard stands are always good, as are trees or standing people. Next, dive down, hold your nose, turn on your back, and look straight up at the surface of the water. You will immediately see the hole described earlier, and in it, hovering directly overhead—instead of off to the side—will be objects you spotted on the shore. This view is a powerful illusion, and the first time you try it, you will find yourself turning your head, looking toward the shore in the direction where you first saw the object you selected. You will try to see objects on the shore, but by looking to the sides of the hole, you will see only the underside of the water's surface. When you come to the surface again, you will find it hard to believe that what you saw overhead a moment ago is now well off to your side, but you will better understand why you see so few large fish as you hike along the water.

If you want to demonstrate at home how water bends light, try this simple experiment. Put a penny into a bowl and lower your head until the penny disappears below the rim of the bowl. Now, while the your head is in this position, slowly pour water into the bowl. As the water fills the bowl, the penny miraculously comes back into view. This magical reappearance occurs because the light is bending around the rim of the bowl, carrying an image of the penny with it. If your penny were a fish in a pond, you would see it even if it were below the shoreline, but remember that it would be able to see you, too. So keep low when you walk along the water and you are sure to see more fish.

In addition to staying low to the ground as you approach the water, you can do a few other things to help increase your chances of spotting fish or other aquatic life. First of all, try to walk so the sun is at your back. This position allows a clear view of the underwater area illuminated by the light rays penetrating the water surface and reduces the glare from reflected light. However, be careful that your shadow does not move across the water and alert the underwater world to your presence.

It is the glare of sunlight on the water that keeps us from seeing what is going on below. We look at the surface of a still pond and see only the reflection of the sky above. Sometimes we just have to accept that this is the way things are, but often, we can refocus our eyes so we see past the reflective surface and down into deeper waters. This is something like looking through the windshield of a car: you see what is up ahead on the road, but you don't notice the windshield itself—you have focused your vision beyond it.

Learning to look through the surface glare improves with practice. Some people can learn to do it right away; others need some time to master the technique. To start, try to see the bottom a little farther out beyond the area where the water is transparent. Stare at the reflective surface and try to focus below it. In no time at all you will begin to see the shapes of rocks, logs, and maybe even a big pickerel or trout lurking just offshore. When the bottom first comes into focus, you will feel as if your eyes have been gifted with a strange new power.

Two other factors are important to the fish watcher. The first is to get as high as possible above the water. If you look down from a tree or a bridge, you will get a view of the bottom that is unequaled from the shore. The second is to be aware of the sounds you make as you approach the water. You can talk as you approach the shore; sound waves in the air do not transfer easily into water. But walk softly. Sound traveling through rock and soil moves easily into water, and the pounding of heavy footsteps on the ground above will send fish diving for deep water or for the cover of some lush garden of aquatic vegetation.

As with all stalking, some places are better for it than others. Knowing these prime environments will help guarantee that you see some fish, which will encourage you to continue looking for them in the future. The following list will give you a general idea of the places fish are most likely to be seen.

Environment	Why Fish Are There
Lakes and Ponds	
Underwater weed beds	Food and protection for small fish; prey for large fish.
Edges of lily pads	Insects on stems provide food for small fish, which then attract large fish; shade.
Mouths of streams entering lakes	Flowing water brings in food and highly oxygenated water.
Protruding points of land	No real benefit, but fish swimming at various distances parallel to the shore are all forced to pass through the area off the tip.
Piers and docks	Weeds and insects on pilings provide food for bait fish; shade.
Rivers and Streams	
Overhanging brush or trees	Food, protection from aerial attack, shade.
Merging currents	More food carried to waiting fish.
Outsides of bends	The outside of a bend in a stream is always deeper, so it offers protection and more food.
Dams and falls	Deep holes below vertical drops of water provide protection. Fish cannot move beyond this point, and those moving upstream to spawn or find cooler water tend to congregate here.
Behind big rocks	Rocks break the force of the current, giving fish in swiftly running streams a place to rest. Also, currents dig holes behind rocks, offering protection and food.

Remember to look into the water whenever you are outdoors. The reward will be a view of fish—and frogs, turtles, snakes, muskrats, and much more—that would have been missed otherwise.

Nesting Materials

*E*very bird nest is a monument to the genius of animal instinct, for each bird builds the same nest as others of its kind, following a blueprint stored deep within its genes.

Yet, even though all nests of a single species are of the same design, each one is unique because it must be constructed with the materials at hand.

We can participate in the lives of birds by influencing the appearance of the nests they build. To do this, collect yarn, string, strips of paper, or anything else you think might make a good nest and hang it outdoors in May or early June. You can place this material on small trees and shrubs, much as tinsel is draped over the branches of a Christmas tree, or you can stuff it all loosely into a mesh bag like the kind onions come in. Soon birds will be landing at this stockpile and flying off again with a length of string or a strip of paper in their beaks. Construction has begun.

Try to keep the birds in sight as they fly away with the material you put out. The ideal time to locate their nesting sites is when they travel back and forth between the supplies you have provided and the nests they are building. Don't worry if you can't locate the nest on the first few tries. Nest building takes several days to a week or more, and each bird will make hundreds of trips to gather the materials it needs.

One never knows what species will come to poke around the piles that have been set out; cardinals, kingbirds, blue jays, and robins can all be expected. Personally, I am always most intrigued when I see a northern oriole pick up a bit of my string or yarn. I know that this bird—always a female—will take what I have offered and weave it into a nest that dangles precariously from the thin branch of a tree, 25 to 30 feet above the ground. For several years in a row, I have found the exact location of the oriole nests in my yard by looking for the strands of bright blue yarn I had set out for these birds. Against the light-green foliage of early spring, these dazzlingly blue threads give away the nest's location every year.

The weave itself holds the oriole's nest together, and there is something about this structure that captures the imagination. It's not unlike the fascination that is kindled by those flimsy rope bridges that span bottomless gorges in every adventure film. No mud mortars the parts together as in the robin's nest, no woody tree trunk or branches shore up the sides. Only the strength of the female oriole's weave keeps her eggs or nestlings from plummeting to the ground. But even though these nests look somewhat flimsy, the oriole's skill in engineering these structures has been passed on from one generation of females to the next over several millennia—the design has been well tested.

The first heavy snow of winter makes it possible for you to make a survey of the number of birds that nested and raised their young in your area. Bird nests, by virtue of their wide, horizontal surfaces, catch the falling snow, which then builds up into small, white mounds. This mound shape can easily be spotted among the leafless branches of winter's trees and shrubs, and you will surely find a few surprises on this bird-nest census.

Some birds have probably nested right under your nose, maybe in a rosebush or in the hedge that borders your lawn. I've never found all of the nests in my yard before the first snow of the season, and when I find one I didn't know about, I always wonder how much we miss as we casually view the world around us, especially when the newly discovered nest has a strand of yarn from my spring stockpile woven into it.

Whistling Woodchucks

Whistle pig, marmot, groundhog, and varmint are all common names for *Marmota monax*, the animal I have always called a woodchuck.

But regardless of the name you call them, these pudgy balls of fur are always delightful to watch as they waddle through a field, stopping here and there to nibble some clover or devour a dandelion.

Woodchucks live throughout most of the eastern United States and Canada, and once you start looking for them, they seem to be everywhere. The reason we see so many is that, unlike most other ground-dwelling mammals, woodchucks are active during the day and usually reside in open areas where you can easily observe them. But while you can easily spot a woodchuck, this animal's keen hearing and vision make it easy for the woodchuck to spot you. If your goal is to observe one of these wary creatures, make only slow movements, keep quiet, and remain at a distance so that you will not threaten the woodchuck and cause it to make a dash for its burrow—an understandable reaction for an animal heavily preyed upon by the fox and the hawk.

When walking in "chuck" country, you may be startled to hear a short, shrill whistle that sounds much like the one some people make by putting two fingers in their mouth and blowing hard. That whistle is a woodchuck alarm call, and it announces your presence to every woodchuck in the area. On hearing this call, a woodchuck will do one of two things: run for its hole or, quite often, stand up on its hind legs and try to get a better view of what all the excitement is about. Hunters have long been aware of this behavior and have learned to mimic the alarm call to persuade woodchucks to stand up and make better targets of themselves.

This old hunting trick is one of the most impressive ways to create a feeling of fellowship with a wild animal, and if you have never learned the art of the two-fingered whistle that so closely resembles the woodchuck alarm call, don't worry, it is really quite simple. First, put the tips of your index fingers together and place them in your mouth with the tip of the tongue resting on top of them. Next, push the fingers upward, rolling your tongue back until you can close your lips on the first knuckle of your fingers. Keeping your lips tightly sealed around your fingers so that no air can escape around the sides, force a brisk stream of air through the triangular space formed by your fingers and lips. It takes some practice, but by sliding your fingers back and forth, you will eventually move them into the right position to create an attention-getting whistle that will call dogs, rouse children, hail taxis, and bring a chuck up out of the grass.

Once you have mastered the two-fingered whistle, try it the next time you are out in an open field or whenever you spot a woodchuck. I first saw someone do this a long time ago on a summer day at the edge of a lush cow pasture. Everything seemed quite peaceful that day, until the screaming, high-decibel whistle made by the farmhand walking next to me punctuated the silence. Within an instant, three wood-chucks popped up from the tall grass and sat on their haunches, look-ing in our direction. The idea of getting these chubby, brown animals to stand on command was mind-boggling, and I could not have been more impressed if my companion had called up gnomes from the netherworld. I never have forgotten that day, nor that technique.

Don't be too concerned if you can't master the two-fingered whistle; almost any style of whistling will raise some chucks. However, I en-courage you to work on developing the loud whistle described above. Not only is this whistle a better imitation of the woodchuck's alarm call, but if it doesn't work and the woodchuck ignores you or scurries off toward its den, you can always give whistling lessons to anyone who is with you. It is something most folks will enjoy.

Often the only sign of a woodchuck's presence is the hole it digs in the ground, for beneath the soil, the woodchuck is truly in its element. Equipped with muscular, thick-boned legs that are its "shovels," the woodchuck loosens the soil with its forepaws and pushes it back with its hind legs. When a load of loose soil builds up behind the wood-chuck, it turns around and pushes the soil out of the tunnel with its head. This method of excavation results in a pile of freshly dug soil at the den entrance—the key field mark used to identify a woodchuck's tunnel. No other North American burrowing animal leaves this earthen doormat to mark the entrance to its home. This mound is the woodchuck's watchtower and sunbathing platform, and the conspicu-ous color of the newly dug soil allows you to spot these dens at a con-siderable distance.

When you have found the entrance to the woodchuck's den, re-member that the crafty woodchuck may be watching you from one of its secret spy-holes. Most people are not aware that every woodchuck den has two different types of entrances: one obvious and one hidden. The main entrance to the den, with its ever-present mound of freshly dug soil, is always easy to spot; but the woodchuck also digs hidden entrances that are much harder to detect. These hidden entrances, called *plunge holes,* are carefully dug from below so that no loose soil marks their location. When peering from these concealed entrances, the woodchuck needs only to poke its head a little above ground to find out what is going on in the area surrounding its den. Look for these hidden spy-holes—they are usually within a few yards of the main entrance and clearly demonstrate how clever animals can be.

When you are done looking for spy-holes, find a rock large enough to wedge snugly into one of the entrances. Once the rock is in place, press an ear to it, and you may be surprised to hear the rapid scratching of the woodchuck's digging. This technique works because sound travels through solid ground far better than it does through the air. Native Americans utilized this same principle when they pressed their ears to the ground to listen for the hoofbeats of nearby horses or buffalo.

On the average, a woodchuck's tunnel is fewer than 4 feet below the surface and about 15 to 20 feet long. Pace off these measurements and you can create a mental picture of what the woodchuck has constructed beneath your feet. Afterward, as you leave the den area, ask any children that might be along if they know the answer to the old, tongue-twisting question: How much wood would a woodchuck chuck if a woodchuck could chuck wood? The answer (which few people seem to know) is as follows: A woodchuck would chuck all the wood a woodchuck could chuck if a woodchuck could chuck wood. After everyone has had a chance to try his or her skill at mastering this mouthful of nonsense, have the entire group chant it in unison several times; it is somewhat hypnotic and lots of fun.

Eyes in the Dark

We humans are creatures of the daylight hours. Diurnal by our very nature, we distrust the darkness and hurry from the forests and fields as night approaches.

Yet as our sense of vision becomes less effective in the dwindling light, our mind automatically shifts its focus from our eyes to our other senses. Suddenly, we are aware of the wind whispering through the trees, the dank smell of the earth, the gurgling of a nearby brook. Night has come, and familiar places seem somehow foreign.

You may be surprised to learn that a human's night vision is almost as good as that of some owls and is better than that of many nocturnal animals that depend more upon their senses of hearing and smell than their sight. However, you must give your eyes at least 15 minutes to become accustomed to the darkness. You need this time so your irises can open wide to let in more light. If you can manage to spend 40 minutes out in the dark before you get started on your nighttime observations, even better. By then, your retinas will be completely adjusted to the dark environment and able to use the available light to its fullest advantage.

There are several tricks for seeing better in the dark, but the most important one is to learn to look a little to one side of the object you want to view. This technique works because our retinas are covered with two types of nerve cells that are named for their shapes: cones and rods. Cone cells are concentrated in the center of the retina, and we use them to see in bright light and in color. Rod cells are concentrated mostly on the peripheral areas of the retina. These cells give us our night vision. By looking to the side of an object, you direct more of its image onto the rod cells, and things that appeared blurry when stared at directly will suddenly come into focus.

A powerful flashlight is always a comfort to have along on a night walk, but that white shaft of light scanning the trail will surely make every animal in the woods keenly aware of your presence. You can overcome this problem by getting a red lens for your light or by covering a clear lens with red cellophane. Either way, you will be able to shine your light directly on many nocturnal animals without scaring them off. This trick works because most nocturnal animals are totally incapable of seeing red light, which is the reason that zoos use red lights in their exhibitions of night environments. Also, the red beam from your flashlight will not affect your own night vision. When you turn it off, you will still see quite well.

Perhaps the most sensational nighttime activity is illuminating the eyes of hidden animals with your light. You can do this without changing the color of the lens since you are not going to try to get very close to the animals. Put the base of your light by your upper lip or forehead and scan the area around you with the beam. Begin close in and move the beam outward in a series of ever-widening semicircles. As the light skims across the ground, it may cause a pair of eyes suddenly to shine in the darkness. You have just made contact with a dog, a cat, or one of the night-loving wild creatures that are active long after most people have gone inside.

Eyeshine is an eerie phenomenon caused by a membrane of reflective cells that lie behind the retinas of many nocturnal animals. This membrane, called the *tapetum,* reflects incoming light back onto the retina and then straight out of the eye in the same direction from which it came. This returning light creates the glowing eyes you see when the beam from your light catches one of these animal's eyes.

I can't really explain just how startling it can be to see a pair of eyes glowing in the dark. I have been surprised several times. One summer night, I was walking home, shining my light into a copse of trees that grew about 20 yards out in an open field. The night was moonless and very dark, so I was shocked when I suddenly found myself staring at five pairs of large, greenish-white eyes glowing in the brush. It took me only a second to realize that I had come upon a herd of white-tailed deer. But if I hadn't known better, I would have been convinced that a band of fiery-eyed demons was lurking in the trees hoping to waylay a solitary traveler.

An animal's eyeshine color can often be a clue to its identity, and the chart below will help you identify some of the common animals whose eyes "glow" when a beam of light hits them. Make note of the color of the eyeshine you see and where you saw it. Then, even if you don't get to see the animal itself, you will still have some idea of what was looking back at you in the night.

Animal	Eyeshine Color
raccoon	bright yellow
opossum	dull orange
skunk	amber
porcupine	deep red
fox	bright white
white-tailed deer	greenish-white
woodcock	glowing red dots
flying squirrel	reddish-orange

If night walks along lonely roads don't sound very appealing, you can find wild creatures with glowing eyes in your own backyard. Again, hold the butt end of the flashlight against your upper lip or forehead and let its beam skim across your lawn and hedges. With a little patience, you will spot two tiny white specks glimmering like diamonds. Move closer and you will see that you have found a wolf spider, an arachnid that hunts by night. The wolf spider's eyeshine is so radiant that at 10 feet away you can pick out its eyes from the bright reflections of raindrops on the ground.

Try a night walk with children. Something about being alone together in the dark brings you closer to one another. As the poet Robert Frost put it: "Every child should have the memory of at least one long-after-bedtime walk."

The Lore of the Tracker

Was it human or animal? How long ago did it pass? Was it running or walking? Traveling with a purpose or rambling?

A footprint, broken twig, or scratch in the moss can tell an experienced tracker all these things—things that the untrained eye would entirely overlook.

The easiest way to learn the fundamentals of tracking is to follow your own footprints. To begin, find an area that is flat, relatively free of vegetation, and has soil soft enough to show at least a partial footprint when you tread upon it. Places such as baseball diamonds and construction sites usually make good training areas.

When you find the right place, mark a point of departure, walk a short distance in a straight line, and return to the spot where you started along a slightly different route. Look down at the first track you made and walk around it in a small circle. As you do, notice how the track is most obvious when it lies between you and the sun and least visible when the sun is at your back. Shadows make the difference in the way a track appears, and because of this, the best time to go tracking is during the morning or late afternoon when the sun is low and the shadows are long. At these times every bump and ridge in a track is highlighted with a border of dark shadow that makes it stand out in contrast to the surrounding soil. This experiment clearly demonstrates the reason why the first rule of tracking is: Always try to keep the trail you are following between the sun and yourself.

As you begin to follow your trail, try to locate each individual track before going on to the next. This procedure is important because the tracks that are hardest to find have the most to teach us. Also, because the clue to locating each new track is contained in the one before it, never destroy the tracks you have already discovered; they are the reference points to which you will return should the trail suddenly "disappear." Experienced trackers always try to situate themselves behind or to the side of the last track they find. In this position, they are in no danger of destroying the trail they are following.

In most tracking situations, an entire footprint will probably not be outlined in the soil. But even though the whole track may not visible, you will be able to see parts of it, and it is the art of finding these fractional footprints that makes tracking so challenging and entertaining.

The most easily recognized fragment of a human track is a general flattening of the ground where a person has stepped. Humans create this sign when the weight of the foot compresses soil, causing it to reflect light differently from the undisturbed ground surrounding it. The weight of a foot will also force pebbles and twigs into the ground, leaving an unnatural gap between these objects and the soil. However, if the foot did not come straight down but struck the ground at an angle, the pebble or twig may be jammed forward or knocked entirely from its bed. Often, these dislodged objects will show a part of themselves that is different in color because they are moist from being underground. They may even have soil clinging to their now-upturned bottoms. This repositioning of materials is important, for it is often the only sign you will find on harder ground.

In addition to tramping down the earth, the human foot also impresses regular geometric lines in the soil that do not normally occur in nature. These unnatural regularities are another easily noticed clue. Sneakers, hiking boots, and most other outdoor footwear all have distinctive patterns on their soles that can help the tracker find a footprint or separate the quarry's track from those of others. But sole designs do not print well on hard ground, so very often you must seek other parts of the footprint.

Perhaps the fragment of a track most frequently found is the crescent-shaped depression formed by the heel of a shoe as it is brought down at the beginning of each step. After flattening, this heel curve is the easiest sign for beginners to find. The indentation formed at the end of a step when the weight is shifted forward and the walker pushes off from the front of the foot is less obvious. These toe digs are not hard to see, but it requires practice to recognize them.

The flattened areas of ground and the impression of unnatural lines and curves on soil are the most noticeable signs of a human's passage through the area, but with practice, you can easily locate other signs. Keep your eyes peeled for bent or bruised vegetation, the lighter interior color of freshly broken twigs, and scuff marks on rocks or moss. Be alert; clues are always there.

Sooner or later, a trail you are following will seem to disappear. You stand behind the last track, staring at the place where the next one should be, yet all you can see is undisturbed ground. When you lose the trail, get down on your hands and knees and face the place where the next track should be. Then lower your ear to the ground and close your uppermost eye. Often, this change of perspective will cause "invisible" tracks to pop right into view. The technique works so well that it will even reveal the prints of bare feet on a linoleum floor.

Another way to locate a vanished trail is to use a tracking stick, a device that measures the average distance between successive footprints.

The stick itself is nothing more than a three- or four-foot walking stick, ski pole, or piece of dowel, but a rubber band slipped over the shaft makes it into a useful tool.

When using a tracking stick, you must first find two consecutive and well-defined tracks. Line up the forward end of the stick with the back edge of the heel mark on the forward track. Then, keeping the forward end in place, slide the rubber band back until it is directly over the heel mark on the rear track. Once this arrangement is set, you will be able to determine exactly where the next heel print should be when you measure from the one before it.

To locate obscure tracks, line up the rubber band with the heel mark of the last track you found, and slowly move the forward end of the tracking stick in an arc. As the stick moves, the tip travels over the area where the next track should appear and focuses your attention there. Suddenly, as if by magic, a crimped blade of grass, a scuff in the soil, or some other minute detail will appear. Everyone feels like a modern-day Sherlock Holmes the first time he or she uncovers one of these tiny clues. It is exhilarating to be able to see what most people would have missed altogether or viewed as inconsequential to the search.

After several practice sessions, bring some friends along. The key to getting them interested is to find soil that makes tracking moderately difficult. This type of soil will challenge them to find the next track, but will not leave them feeling frustrated. When they have learned what basic signs to look for and the use of a tracking stick, they will be ready to play Tracks to the Treasure. This game involves a track maker (you) who lays down a winding trail of 25 steps, which the trackers (your friends) follow, finding at least one sign for each footprint, until they come to a track with an X drawn through it. This game is a challenging way to develop observational skills and a novel way to spend an afternoon.

If you become interested in tracking, learn to identify the paw prints of the larger mammals that inhabit the area. It is always a thrill to find tracks that reveal where a raccoon was fishing in a nearby stream, or the path a fox took as it trotted across a field in the night. Tracking will give you a way to become familiar with the secret lives of wild animals and can stimulate your imagination. After all, somewhere up ahead, at the very end of every trail, an animal's paw is resting in the last track.

A Bird in the Palm

Years ago, while tramping through the woods after an especially long snowstorm, I stopped to smoke my pipe and enjoy the vast silence of winter. As I brushed some snow off a fallen tree and made myself comfortable, a half dozen black-capped chickadees landed on the branches nearby.

I wasn't particularly interested in them at first and continued digging through my pockets for matches. Then my fingers jammed into a doughnut I had brought along as a snack, smashing it. It was a mess, and I was about to turn the pocket inside out when the old Johnny Appleseed legend popped into my mind. Here was my chance to befriend these little creatures just as that old, pioneer orchardist had over a century ago.

Carefully, I gathered some crumbs from my pocket and in a slow, smooth gesture, stretched out my arm and opened my hand to show the birds the delicacy I was offering. I didn't have long to wait, for in less than a minute, one of the birds was on my thumb, pecking away at the crumbs as fast as it could. In another instant, a second bird was feeding on my hand and a third landed on my forearm. They must have been famished.

Having these 5-inch bundles of feathers rest on my hand is something I will never forget. How light they were. How gentle their grasp. How precisely the line that divided their black caps from their white cheeks was drawn. These are images that are still clear today, 30 years later. At that moment, I made up my mind never to miss an opportunity to hand-feed these birds.

I've repeated this feat several times, but I've discovered that chickadees, bold as they are, will come directly to a stranger's hand only when they are very hungry. For hand-taming during better times, you must get to know the birds and become a sort of "friend of the family." Fortunately, it's quite easy to make the acquaintance of chickadees, and if you have a bird feeder, you are already halfway there.

Winter mornings are the best time to tend your feeder. Birds are hungrier then and are willing to take more chances. To attract chickadees, put out some sunflower seeds, shelled peanuts, chopped walnuts, or doughnut crumbs. Feed the birds every day to let them become used to eating at your feeder and seeing you around. After the birds have been coming to your feeder for about a week, take the food away one morning, and around an hour later, put a little bit back on the feeder. Then step away and wait until the chickadees return to eat.

When the birds arrive, grab a handful of seeds or crumbs and slowly walk up to the feeder. The birds will fly away, but usually they will not disappear from sight. Now, moving slowly and smoothly, lay your open hand on the feeder, showing the birds the small pile of seeds in your palm. This is a critical moment, so you must be very still.

You may not attract any birds the first time you try, but certainly within a few days, one brave chickadee will land on the feeder and feast on the food that is near your hand. Once the food near your hand is gone, and your courageous bird realizes you mean it no harm, it will hop up onto your hand and begin to feed. At this point, when the bird is actually eating out of your hand, you will be very close to hand-taming it. However, things may still go wrong, so always move slowly and be patient.

During the first few times a bird is feeding from your hand, you should take care not to stare directly at it. Predators do this before they strike, so the birds are quite wary of having two big eyes glaring at them. Also, you will find that the birds become nervous if you swallow (another prestrike behavior of predators), so wear a scarf to cover your throat during these initial feedings.

You can always tell if your chickadee is frightened by watching its stomach. If it suddenly begins to throb, something is scaring the bird. When you see this throbbing, stop whatever it is you are doing and wait for the bird to calm down. This is especially important when you begin to move about with your birds. The first time you try to move, their stomachs will start moving in and out rapidly. Take your time and stop when you see this happening. Soon you will be able to move around as freely as you want, but there is one thing you must not do: never try to close your hand and capture your new friend. For whether you succeed in grasping it or not, it will have learned that your open hand is not a safe haven but a waiting trap. The bird will no longer trust you, and when it flies away, it may never return.

Throughout the entire hand-feeding process, you should talk to your birds in soft, conversational tones. A relaxed human voice seems to calm them, and if you always say the same words in the same tone when you first give them food, you can use these words to call them whenever you want. There is nothing like watching a wild bird fly from the bush and make a beeline for your hand.

With more time and patience you also can hand-tame tufted titmice, blue jays, and numerous other birds using sunflowers seeds and peanut hearts. Hand-feeding birds is extremely satisfying, and children who have done this are unlikely to neglect the needs of wildlife as they grow older. For they will never forget that one time, when they were young, a small, soft, and warm creature trusted them and ate in the safety of their outstretched hands.

Calling the Wild

At a very basic level, the ancient art of animal calling is one of those simple pleasures that is entertaining, easy to learn, and quite useful.

You don't need any equipment, just some patience and the ability to stay still. But if you do it right, this activity can greatly increase the number of birds you will see on an outing and will give you a chance to communicate with animals of a different species.

The most common method of calling is known as *squeaking* and has been used by generations of bird-watchers and hunters to lure animals from their hiding places. The squeaking sound is made by lightly pressing your lips to the back of your hand and sucking in, much as if you were mimicking a greatly exaggerated kiss. Each squeak should be only three to five seconds long, and the caller should wait silently for at least one minute before trying again. A longer wait might be even better, but since most birds respond during the first minute, you can repeat the squeak if you find yourself losing interest. Try to add a sense of urgency to the call, but don't overdo it or the animals will become suspicious.

Catbirds, blue jays, song sparrows, mockingbirds, towhees, scarlet tanagers, brown thrashers, titmice, chickadees, and many other birds respond to squeaking, but the response varies by species, season, and the mood of the birds. Overall, this technique seems to work best in the spring and autumn. However, even during late summer, when birds are generally quieter and more reclusive, the frenzied sound of a well-crafted squeak can bring several of them out of hiding.

If the back-of-the-hand technique doesn't work, try making the squeaking sound by "kissing" your palm. This action tends to produce a deeper, louder sound that some larger birds find more attractive. I have also lured numerous birds into the open by gently kissing one of the raised knuckles that form when the hand is made into a fist. The technique creates a soft, imploring call that sounds like the chirping of nestling birds or the twitter of some small rodent.

No one knows for sure why songbirds respond to squeaking. They may be curious, or the sound may closely imitate the distress calls of other birds and small animals. But while the reason for a songbird's response remains unclear, there is no question why predatory animals such as coyotes, foxes, raccoons, owls, and house cats respond: the noise sounds like an easy meal.

From a concealed position, try squeaking when a hawk is flying overhead or when the family cat passes. If you are well hidden, these carnivores will often alter their course to investigate the source of the sound. Many different predators can be lured by squeaking, but they are cautious and take their time—moving in under cover, listening, looking, and sniffing the air. You must stay upwind and be patient, well hidden, and very still if you want to fool one of these wary creatures.

Because so many different species of birds and other animals respond to squeaking, surprising things can happen. Once, while trying to squeak an unidentified bird out of the foliage, I was astonished to see a small, nut-brown head poke out from a hollow stump a short distance away. I wasn't sure what the creature was at first, but when the white chest and long, slim body came into view, I knew I had something in sight that human beings rarely see: a long-tailed weasel. I remained still and silent as the weasel moved toward me with that undulating gait that is the hallmark of the species. When he was within eight feet of my hideout, close enough for me to see the twitching of his nose, a light breeze carried my scent his way, and the only wild weasel I ever saw at close range darted off in a blur of motion and disappeared into the underbrush. Since then, I always put my hand to my mouth and try a few squeaks when I sit down to rest—you never know who is in the neighborhood.

Bird-watchers use another technique to flush birds from hiding. It is called *pishing* and consists of a series of whistlelike hisses that mimic the calls many smaller species use while scolding an owl, cat, or other predator. The call is simple. You make an intense, rhythmic *pssh* … *pssh* … *pssh* … sound by forcing a stream of air through clenched teeth.

An entire series of these calls should last about 3 or 4 seconds and should be followed by a period of silence lasting at least 30 seconds. This call has no exact rhythm, so you should experiment to find the one that works best. Listen for birds making the *pssh* sound when you are outdoors because there is no better model than the real thing. Besides, something interesting is happening at the place that sound is coming from, something that may be worth investigating.

I have flushed an untold number of birds from hedges and thick brush using this technique, and I have used it to lure wrens, warblers, nuthatches, catbirds, kinglets, and numerous other birds to my position. Once the *pssh* call enticed a ruby-throated hummingbird away from a blossoming columbine and brought it to hover directly over my sleeping bag. It was there only for a moment, but the memory of the bird's bright iridescence and of the sound of its humming wings has lasted for decades.

When calling birds, always remain very quiet and still. Also, you should make an effort to keep yourself at least partially concealed. Most birds have good eyesight and can easily recognize the outline of the human form. By hiding behind some brush or the trunk of a tree, you will break up your silhouette and increase the chances of success.

Those readers interested in knowing more about the sounds they hear when they walk in the woods should obtain a recording of common birdcalls. With one of these recordings, you can listen to an individual call over and over until you know it well enough to recognize it in the field. Sadly, most people cannot recognize the call of the common robin and believe that all birdsongs are akin to the chirping of a parakeet.

During the spring or early summer, when birds are most vocal, memorize several common calls and go out on a birdsong scavenger hunt. If you begin with calls of abundant birds such as the robin, yellowthroat, or white-throated sparrow, your success will be guaranteed, and you will be encouraged to learn the calls of other, less common species.

Another reason to learn birdcalls is that many male birds respond quickly to the territorial calls of their own kind. In fact, due to the strong reaction of male birds to rivals, it is relatively easy to attract rose-breasted grosbeaks, northern orioles, bobwhites, cardinals, and numerous other species by imitating their calls. Again, the records will help you develop this skill.

Learning to hear and recognize wild voices will change the way you experience nature and add a new depth to your understanding and appreciation of the immediate environment. With practice, you will no longer be limited to sensing only those creatures the eye can see, but you will learn the tales that every peep, cheep, buzz, trill, and hoot has to tell about the wild residents of the woods and fields.

Sense Enhancement

People see only what they choose to look at, and they look at only what they think is important. Every human being views the world this way, and this explains why urbanites rarely look at the tops of skyscrapers and why botanists always see more flowers than do ornithologists.

Perhaps the best thing people can do to increase their appreciation of the natural world is to learn how to use their eyes in new ways, ways that let them see more of the world that surrounds them. There are numerous techniques that can be used to bring about a change in perception and perspective, but the easiest to learn is what I call *wide-angle vision.*

Wide-angle vision differs from normal vision not in how you use your eyes, but in where you direct your attention. Using normal vision, you focus your attention on only a small area directly in front of yourself, ignoring your peripheral vision. In wide-angle vision, however, you direct your attention throughout the entire field of vision. You see everything but do not concentrate on any one part of it.

Next time you go outdoors, try being conscious of everything in your field of vision while looking straight ahead. Almost instantly, the scene before your eyes will seem to grow "softer" as your attention spreads out. Notice how things off to the side and up in the trees become more conspicuous, and how every motion in the landscape seems to catch your eye. If the grass sways, you see it; if a leaf wiggles, you spot it; if an animal moves, it is under your gaze. As soon as you see something of interest, your mind automatically triggers the eyes to focus on it so you can study it in detail. You may not be able to maintain wide-angle vision for very long during your first few attempts, so try regularly to slip in and out of it until you can do it comfortably. Soon, seeing this way will become a matter of habit.

Wide-angle vision will not only help you spot more wildlife, it will also increase your general awareness of the area around you. Try scanning your entire field of vision to see how everything fits together, or search for a specific shape or color. You will be surprised to find out how well the human mind can both harmonize the diverse elements of a landscape and extract its subtle details. Older children learn this skill with remarkable speed. They seem to be able to break out of the "things-are-as-they-are" world of adults, yet have adequate mental control to learn the technique.

In contrast to the wide-angle technique, the field of vision can also be narrowed to create a new awareness of one's surroundings by using a method called *tight-framing.* Scan an area along some change in the terrain such as a shoreline, a ridgeline, the edge of a wood, or a rock wall, and try to remember everything you see. Next, slowly scan the same landscape through the center of the ring formed by curling the index finger down to meet the thumb. The results are usually quite surprising. For many things that were missed during the first observation pop into view when you narrow the visual field and pay greater attention to each segment of the landscape. This technique is an excellent way to spot animals and flowers and can help anyone who is "it" play a far better game of hide-and-seek.

Tight-framing can also help you become more aware of the miniature world that often disappears when using the normal scale of vision. This time, curl the index finger down until it almost bends back against itself. This finger position will leave a tiny hole at the center of the curled finger, which extremely reduces the field of vision and focuses the attention on a very small area. Suddenly, you will notice things that you previously overlooked: a drop of dew on a stone, or an aphid on a plant stem. This tiny hole is second only to a magnifying glass in revealing the smaller side of nature, and I have even spotted amoebas in pond water using this technique.

Modern living has also taught people to filter out much of the sound in their environment, perhaps because there is always too much of it. For the most part, filtering unnecessary sound is beneficial and allows urbanites to ignore much of the noise that is constantly bombarding their ears. But when these city dwellers get a chance to spend some time in the woods, this filtering ability becomes a serious handicap and causes them to miss much of what is happening around them. They don't lack the auditory ability or the desire to hear these sounds; instead, they have become too rushed to listen closely for a gurgling brook or for the wind in the pines.

The best way to restimulate your awareness of the sounds around you is to learn how to increase the sensitivity of your ears. Look at a rabbit or deer and ask yourself if the big ears perched prominently on these animals' heads have anything to do with their excellent sense of hearing. The answer is obvious. Big ears are more effective sound-gathering structures than small ears, and you can easily demonstrate this fact by "increasing" the size of your own ears.

To begin, close your eyes and pick out a soft, steady sound such as the wind in the trees or a small animal rustling in the leaves. Listen intently for a moment, and then cup your hands behind your ears and push the outer ear forward with the thumb and index finger. This movement is exactly the same as the gesture that you make when you can't hear what someone is saying, and it will make whatever you are listening to sound louder, almost as if someone had turned up the volume. In fact, if you want to try this trick at home, turn down the volume on the television or radio until you hear the sound but not the words from across the room. Next, cup your hands behind your ears and listen. With your hands in this "big ear" position, you will easily recognize the individual words.

After learning the big ear technique, find a chirping cricket, a singing bird, or some other noisy animal. It is far easier to locate the source of this sound with your hands cupped around your ears. Listen to the wind as it moves through the leafless branches of the winter woods, then close your eyes and cup your hands around your ears. Suddenly, your hearing will go beyond the general rustling and will begin to pick out the tap of twigs knocking against one another and the rusty hinge–creaking of the tree trunks. This technique will make you aware of the importance of listening and will teach you that there are no soloists in nature, only myriad voices singing in an infinite chorus.

Wide-angle vision, tight-framing, and big ears are activities that can help anyone gain a better awareness of the natural world. Try these techniques in your "home" woods, or any other place with which you are intimate. You will be amazed when you discover how much we neglect in the places we frequent the most.

The Blue Jay Illusion

Something always watches you when you walk in the woods. Even if you don't see a thing, there are eyes, ears, and noses straining to determine your intentions. It is the way of wild things.

As a rule, most animals are shy and will run and hide as soon as they detect you. But every woods has a few self-appointed sentinels that feel it is their duty to alert every creature within earshot to the fact of your presence. The most common and clamorous of these criers is the blue jay, a bird with splendid plumage, a spunky attitude, and a strident voice. Next time you are out walking, listen for a loud, metallic, *jaay-jaay* sound. This sound is the most common of all blue jay calls, and the birds use it to alert other jays, warning them of the approach of danger or rallying them to mob a predator.

Jays chide cats, foxes, weasels, hawks, and owls as soon as they spot them. But the blue jay doesn't exclude two-legged intruders, and if you are walking in an area that humans do not normally frequent, the blue jays will quickly give away your position. So next time you hear a jay calling out, look around; it may be that you are the subject of all this fuss.

Other animals listen for the jay's alarm calls and take notice when they hear them. Birds become silent as deer perk up their ears and look in the direction of the call. There is even a case on record of a porcupine erecting its quills just because it heard a jay calling. If you doubt the effect of the jay's alarm call on other animals, ask any hunter about it. They will all tell you that game animals get quite skittish when some pesky blue jay starts making a racket.

In the wild, blue jays feed mostly on vegetable matter, with a strong preference for acorns. They spend a great deal of time collecting and burying these heavy seeds in the autumn, and they are so ambitious in this endeavor that some scientists believe jays may have been the reason oak trees, after the last ice age, spread northward more quickly than many trees having small, wind-borne seeds.

Beyond the jay's preference for nuts and seeds, it is a very opportunistic feeder and will gobble up whatever it can get. Insects make up a large part of its diet, but frogs, salamanders, fish, berries, spiders, snails, and even bats have been found in the birds' stomachs. Occasionally, blue jays will raid the nests of other songbirds and feed on the eggs or nestlings they find there. It is a rare occurrence, yet it has brought about a widespread dislike of this resourceful bird. Chipmunks, squirrels, raccoons, and cats all do the same thing, but we humans are selective in our moralizing; and perhaps the blue jay is simply too brash for our liking.

The intensely blue plumage of the blue jay is one of the most amazing things about this intriguing bird. Yet, as vivid as this color is, it is not real. For in all the world, no blue birds exist whose color is truly caused by pigments in the feathers.

Birds such as the blue jay, the bluebird, and the indigo bunting all get their brilliant blue coloration from the scattering and reflection of light—the same way as the ocean and sky. This fact is quite startling when you first hear it, but is really quite simple in operation. Essentially, the blue jay's feathers act as a prism. When light strikes one of these birds, a colorless layer of cells just below the upper surface of the feathers splits the light up and reflects the blue wavelengths back toward the eyes of the beholder. All of the other colors of the spectrum pass through this layer and are absorbed by another, darkly pigmented cell layer that lies below.

The prismatic quality of blue jay feathers is a good way to demonstrate how things are not always exactly what they appear to be. Pick up one of these feathers and note its bright-blue color. Then hold it up toward the sun, and, immediately, it will appear to be light gray instead of brilliant blue. The light is not hitting the feather in a way that permits the blue to be reflected to your eyes. This experiment should remind us of how one's perspective can change the way things appear—a lesson to be remembered when judging the blue jay by its feeding habits.

Interacting with Insects, Spiders, & Worms

Talking to Fireflies

*E*ach year, early in the summer, the flashing lights of the season's first fireflies lure thousands of children from their houses. Running this way and that, the children try to capture the twinkling insects in an empty jar. It's a ritual that has gone on for generations.

As you probably already know, only the male firefly can fly, and he is the one you see darting back and forth across your lawn, flashing out his courtship message to the wingless female who waits in the grass or shrubs below. What you may not know is that there are several different species of firefly, each with its own flash pattern that may differ in color, intensity, or timing of the light. In fact, individual species can differ even in the time of night and altitude at which they flash. In the mating game of fireflies, the male's flash must be exactly right in every way or the female will not respond.

One of the most common fireflies is *Photinus pyralis* (there are no common names for the different firefly species), and early each summer evening you can find this insect flashing its light above the open fields and lawns of eastern North America. The signal of this firefly is recognizable because it always rises upward as it flashes its bright, yellow light. This rising pattern is formed because *Photinus pyralis* always flies in an undulating manner and flashes only while it is ascending. At sunset, this firefly flashes low to the ground, but as the evening wears on, it will soar somewhat higher, continuing to emit its identifying J-shaped flashes.

The actual flash code of *Photinus pyralis* is quite simple and is based on the time that elapses between its burst of light and the female's response. While flying, the male gives off a series of flashes about six seconds apart. The female, who is located down in the grass, will then flash a response about two seconds after the male's signal. When the male sees this, he flies toward the female, and the two continue this sequence of flashes until they are together.

You can join this "romantic" conversation and lure a male *Photinus pyralis* to your hand by imitating the luminous response of a female. All you need to do is take a small flashlight and go to a place where you see the J-shaped flashes of this firefly. As soon as you spot one of the flashes, start counting off two seconds (one Mississippi ... two Mississippi), and then, holding the flashlight close to the ground, turn it on for about one second. Almost immediately, the male will turn and head toward your light. When he flashes again, give him another quick flash of your light after waiting the proper two seconds. Continue this responsive flashing, and the firefly will keep moving closer. As it nears you, its flashes will become much weaker. Keep flashing your light, and in no time at all, the male will land directly on your hand or alight nearby and walk to your light.

If you have only a large flashlight, you can still perform this trick by keeping the lens of the light almost flat on the ground. When you see the male flashing, tilt your light up a little on the side that faces him and give it a flash. He will come in.

I have brought in male *Photinus pyralis* from over 40 feet away, and it can quickly become a neighborhood fad. However, make sure you remind everyone that the flashlights should be put away when they finish using them. More than once I have found my light in the grass as I left for work in the morning.

If *Photinus pyralis* doesn't frequent your backyard, there is another activity you can enjoy using any species of firefly: the flash accelerator. As I mentioned earlier, kids love to put fireflies in jars; yet, they don't know what to do with the creatures once they have captured them. While children may not realize it, by imprisoning fireflies in glass, they have provided all that is needed to perform a most curious activity.

First, have the children note how fast their captured fireflies are flashing or ask them to count the seconds between the flashes of some free-flying males. Next, dip the jar containing the fireflies into a pot of lukewarm water. As the temperature inside the jar begins to rise, your fireflies will begin to flash faster and faster. Soon you will notice that the insects in the jar are giving off several flashes for every one emitted by the fireflies still flying freely about the yard.

The reason for this change in flash rate is simple: a firefly's flashing is affected by the temperature of the air surrounding it. The higher the temperature, the shorter the period between flashes. With *Photinus pyralis,* for example, the interval between flashes is about eight seconds at 65°F and four seconds at 82°F. You can make the fireflies flash even faster, but first a word of warning. Many children (and adults) mistakenly believe that if warm is good, hot must be better. Following this theory, they immerse the jar in near-boiling tap water, only to find that their little captives have curled up their legs and fallen unconscious to the bottom of the jar. You should never create conditions so extreme that these creatures become overwhelmed by the heat. Instead, always raise the temperature gradually by adding more warm water to the pot. By doing this, I have had some local species flashing like miniature strobe lights and have created an event that the kids enjoyed night after night.

When you have finished playing with the fireflies, open the jar and let the insects fly away to add their bright magic to the night landscape. There is no reason to keep them until morning. As the Japanese say, "By day a firefly is only an insect, but at night it becomes something else." What does it become? A miracle.

The Ant Parade

When you look at a single ant foraging near your feet, you cannot help but wonder how such a tiny creature can find enough to eat each day.

The truth of the matter is that no ant forages for itself; it feeds, and is fed by, its colony. The individual ant is only a single cell in a greater body, a cell so designed for communal life that it is born with two stomachs: one for itself and another larger one to hold food for its fellows. To feed their nest-mates, ants transfer liquid food to one another mouth-to-mouth, and experiments have shown that if one ant is fed on radioactively marked food, that radioactivity will be detected in the bodies of every other ant in the colony before one day passes.

Watch an ant as it forages. Notice how the two long antennae, which are both fingers and nose to the ant, are constantly moving and touching everything in their path. When the ant finds some tidbit lying on the ground, a remarkable sequence of events begins. First, the ant tastes its discovery. Then, it turns around and heads directly back to its nest, marking the trail with a chemical it excretes from its abdomen. The chemical marker, technically called a *pheromone*, will excite the ant's nest-mates and recruit them to follow the scent trail back to the newly discovered food. Every ant that follows the scent and feeds on whatever the first ant found will add more pheromone to the trail as it returns to the nest. This makes the scent trail even stronger and entices more workers to leave the nest and gather in the food. Soon there is a procession of ants moving both ways along the trail between the food and the nest.

To demonstrate that the ants are following a scent, and not just marching behind one another, run your finger across their path, roughing up the soil. The next ant to arrive at the rub mark you made will act quite confused. It will move from side to side and even backward trying to pick up the trail you erased by removing the pheromone with your finger. After much scouting around, the lost ant will eventually reconnect the trail you have disturbed and go back to the business of gathering food for the colony.

The scent trail also tells the ants when it is no longer worth traveling to a feeding site. As the food runs out, more and more ants turn around and head back to the nest without feeding. These unsuccessful foragers leave no scent as they return, so the strength of the scent trail diminishes and fewer ants are drawn to follow it. Eventually, all of the food will be consumed and none of the returning ants will mark the trail. After a short period of time, the pheromones that were laid down earlier evaporate and the trail will disappear.

Woodpile
Acrobats

Along with the ever-present field mouse and gardens of fungi, woodpiles house three miniature acrobats who will entertain everyone. These acrobats are all very different from one another, perform entirely different tricks, and, fortunately, are easy to find and safe to handle.

The first of these Lilliputian entertainers is the click beetle, which, for its size, can outjump crickets, grasshoppers, rabbits, and even the largest kangaroos. The most amazing thing of all is that this high-jumping insect doesn't even use its legs. In fact, it prepares for its startling leaps by lying on its back!

Ten thousand species of click beetle exist throughout the world, and about 800 of these live in North America. The beetles vary in appearance and size, but in general, they are less than two inches long and tend to be slender, smooth, and shiny. While click beetles all look somewhat different, one thing they all have in common is a long protrusion that extends from the front segment of their bodies down into a socket in the rear segment. This structure gives the click beetle both its name and its acrobatic ability.

If you pick up a click beetle with your fingers, the first thing it may do is snap its body back and forth, making a loud *click* with every movement. Often this maneuver surprises people and enables the beetles to escape their grasp. After all, nobody expects that much wiggle and noise from a small insect. Such a reaction is exactly what nature intended, because this animated behavior is sometimes enough to startle a bird or lizard into releasing a click beetle it has captured. This noise-making ability is the inspiration for some of the click beetle's other common names such as snapper or snapping beetle.

If you flip a click beetle on its back, it will perform one of the great stunts of the insect world. After lying motionless for a few moments, the beetle will kick its legs, push its middle up, and with another *click,* attempt to right itself by somersaulting several inches into the air.

It is the protrusion and socket located on the beetle's underside that gives the beetle its phenomenal jumping ability. When the protrusion, or *peg,* as it is sometimes called, is in an "uncocked" position, it reaches down from the front segment and fits neatly into a socket in the rear section. When the beetle finds itself on its back or in something's mouth, it arches its midsection upward, which lifts the peg up and locks its tip onto a lip located slightly forward of the socket. With the peg wedged securely against this lip, the beetle then contracts the large muscles on its ventral side until the extreme tension snaps the peg off the lip with a jolt that flings the insect into the air.

Although a click beetle's leaps are usually completely vertical and totally uncontrolled, the airborne beetle always manages to flip at least once in the air. Unfortunately, this insect acrobat is just as likely to come down again on its back as on its feet. But click beetles are tenacious little creatures, and in a moment or so, another *click* will be heard as the beetle relaunches itself skyward. Sometimes these insects will right themselves with their legs. If they do, turn them over again. You won't have to try many times to get this little acrobat to give a performance.

Click beetles are found throughout the United States, and if you don't have a woodpile nearby, look for them around old stumps or rotted logs. These beetles are also attracted to bright lights at night, so you may be able to pluck one right off the wall under a porch light. As soon as you identify your catch as a click beetle, call anyone you know who still has their sense of wonder. Then, flip the beetle on its back and ask them to watch it closely. You should watch your audience instead of the insect, because when the beetle lifts off for the first time, you will know from the looks on their faces that something they will never forget has happened.

The eyed elater *(Alaus oculutus)* is perhaps the most spectacular of all North American click beetles. This rather large (one- to two-inch), gray-black beetle has two large black spots on its back that look like eyes. While these eyespots are meant to scare predators into thinking the insect is larger than it really is, they also make eyed elaters easy to identify. Have the children pick up these beetles and turn them on their backs. As is the case with all click beetles, eyed elaters don't bite and are always ready to put on a show. If the children want to take the beetles home for a while, instruct them to keep their new pets in a terrarium with some decayed wood or fruit to eat. Click beetles do well in captivity, but as with all wild pets, you should release them into suitable habitats after a short period of observation.

The second star performer of the woodpile is the harvestman, or daddy longlegs. Common throughout most of the United States, these gangly creatures are usually mistaken for members of the spider family. This mistake is easy to make, for both spiders and harvestmen have small bodies and walk about on eight long, skinny legs. But a closer look reveals some noticeable differences. The most obvious distinction between the two is that a spider's body is always divided into two parts, while the body of the harvestman is all one piece. In addition, a spider can spin silk from special glands in its body, the harvestman cannot. From a strictly scientific standpoint, harvestmen and spiders belong to the same class of animals (Arachnida), but harvestmen are of the order Opiliones, while all North American spiders belong to the orders Orthognatha and Labidognatha.

Perhaps the most important difference between spiders and harvestmen is that while some spiders bite, all harvestmen are completely harmless and safe to hold in your hands. However, if you want to hold one, be gentle and never try to pick up one of these creatures with your fingers. If you do, the harvestman may jettison a leg or two that will wiggle in your hands while your specimen escapes back into the woodpile. The harvestman will survive the loss of these legs; they are meant to come off and distract predators by their movement. But unlike many spiders, harvestmen cannot grow the missing limbs back again. Instead of trying to grasp one of these "breakable" creatures, gently guide it on to your hand or arm and let it walk around until you can get it into a container.

When a harvestman has been captured, sit down on the grass and let it loose. Have you ever seen a more ungainly animal? It looks like a brown pea that bounces along on legs made of bent cat whiskers. However, this creature is well adapted to its environment. With those long, lanky legs, a harvestman can move quite quickly, often walking across the tops of tall blades of grass. In its own way, it travels something like Tarzan, moving above the jungle floor on an aerial skyway, never touching the ground.

If you look closely at harvestmen, you will notice that their second pair of legs is longer than the others and always seems to be waving around out in front. As is true for most things in nature, there is a good reason for this behavior: the tips of those legs contain the harvestman's organs of taste, touch, hearing, and smell, and it uses them to explore its surroundings. Clap your hands or make some other loud noise in front of the harvestman and it will immediately jerk those two long legs backward. Take a moment to imagine what it would be like to hear with your hands, or, stranger yet, to taste with your fingers.

Harvestmen perform one acrobatic stunt that resembles that of the sky diver, for these creatures can fall from great heights and, like cats, always land on their feet. Unlike cats, however, no matter how far a harvestman falls, it will walk away unhurt—its entire body is a natural parachute.

To demonstrate this high-diving ability, guide a harvestman onto the palm of your hand and strike the back of that hand, launching the harvestman into the air. Instantly, the eight-legged aerialist will freeze in its normal position (with the body held well below the bent elbows of its legs) and float gently to earth. This position, combined with the light weight of the harvestman, guarantees a slow descent and a safe, upright landing. Harvestmen frequently use this jump-and-float-to-the-ground behavior as a method of escape, and it is quite natural for them. The only danger is that once children have tried this stunt, they will want to launch harvestmen from higher and higher places. No danger exists for the harvestmen, but keep an eye on the kids.

The last woodpile entertainer is the pill bug or wood louse, and although its act is not as dynamic as the click beetle's or the harvestman's, it never fails to bring *oohs* and *aahs* from the mouths of a young audience. These gray, half-inch creatures look like armored beans, and even though they are land-dwelling cousins of the lobster, they appear to have more in common with an armadillo.

What does this diminutive crustacean have to do with an armadillo? The moment you pick one up the resemblance is obvious: both of these armored animals roll themselves up into a protective ball when they face a dangerous situation. This behavior, called *conglobation*, is so similar in these two species that early taxonomists named the pill bug's biological family Armadillididae even though there is absolutely no relationship between pill bugs and armadillos.

The pill bug can utilize this rolled-up defense because it has a flat underside and a hemispherical back covered with a series of overlapping armor plates. When danger threatens, the pill bug arches its back and brings the flat bottoms of the head and tail together. In this position, its armored back forms a barrier against predators.

When no one is looking, pick up a pill bug and lightly jiggle it in your hand—an action that will cause the pill bug to roll up and remain motionless. Then stretch out your hand and announce that you have found a "magic marble." This news should bring every child around to stare at the small, gray ball in the center of your palm. Within a few seconds (pill bugs are obligingly impatient), the magic marble will open and fourteen little legs will begin to thrash in the air until the pill bug rights itself and walks away. This bit of chicanery never fails to capture the imagination of younger children, all of whom will want to find magic marbles of their own.

Finding pill bugs is quite easy, for they seem to live under almost every fallen tree, flat rock, and woodpile in the temperate regions of

North America. However, their look-alike cousin, the sow bug, lives there, too. Neither one of these creatures is harmful in any way, but the sow bug cannot roll itself into a ball. To distinguish pill bugs from other species, look at the tail end of the specimen you are about to capture. If it has tiny tails, it is probably a sow bug; if it appears to be tailless, it is a pill bug and you can let the show begin.

Click beetles, harvestmen, and pill bugs all possess very amusing and entertaining talents; however, always remember that these are living creatures and deserve to be handled gently. Don't work one specimen until it is exhausted; let it do its trick once or twice and then let it go. Kindness toward living creatures and a sense of caring for the earth should be at the heart of every outdoor activity.

Water Walkers

There are around 80 species of water striders in North America, and all are endowed with three pairs of marvelous legs that allow them to walk on water.

If you look closely at the water surface surrounding one of these legs, you will see that the weight of the insect has caused a small depression—the surface of the water is bent but it does not break.

The water supports the water strider because the molecules at the surface are more tightly bound together than those below, causing what is known as *surface tension*. This is the same phenomenon that allows a carefully placed needle to float on the surface of water in a glass, and these insects are well adapted to take advantage of this situation. The water strider's long legs spread its body weight over a large area, and each leg is tipped with waterproof hairs to increase the number of points that come in contact with the water. These adaptations assure that there is never enough pressure at any one point to cause the water strider to break through the surface.

Each pair of a water strider's legs serves the insect in a different way. The front legs are short and are used for support and grasping prey. The middle legs, which are longer than the water strider's entire body, are used as oars to propel the insect across the water. The hind legs are used as rudders to allow the water strider to steer.

When a water strider decides to move, it gives a backward push with its middle pair of legs. But what does it push against if its legs are made to slide over water? Why doesn't it just stay in one place "spinning its wheels"? Ask these questions of your companions; you will be amazed by the theories a human mind can devise. Actually, the answer is quite simple. The water strider gets its forward thrust by pushing against the back wall of the depression formed by the weight of its middle legs on the water. This action creates small waves, but the insect will not break through the surface. In fact, the water strider can leap several inches into the air with one of these thrusts and still not break the surface. One of the most fascinating aspects of water strider movement is that while this initial push creates ripples, the following glide does not. Watch for this. It is intriguing.

The same surface tension that supports the water strider is a clinging trap for most other insects. A moth touching the water's surface will find itself stuck there, and in its struggle to get free, it will send a series of ripples across the water. Water striders can read the message these ripples tell and use them to pinpoint the moth's location.

In order to find its prey, a water strider uses its two front legs as a homing device. If the incoming ripples strike the insect's left leg first, it turns to the left. Ripples reaching both front legs at the same time mean the target is dead ahead. If the water strider isn't sure which direction the ripples are coming from, it turns its body so it can get a better reading from the next set of ripples.

This homing ability gives us an opportunity to trick a water strider into coming right up close to us. Find two thin twigs, each about four or five inches long, and hold the end of one of them just below the surface of the water. Next, draw the other twig back and forth over the one that is partially submerged in the same way a fiddler moves his bow across the strings of his fiddle. This action sets up vibrations in the water that mimic those of an insect in distress, and if any hungry water striders are in the area, they will head straight for the vibrating stick.

The last time I tried "fiddling" for water striders was during autumn, after the leaves had fallen and the abundance of summer insects had passed. Almost immediately after I started, two water striders darted across the pool and grabbed on to my stick. At times like this, when the insects are really hungry, you might be able to lure them by simply flicking a tiny piece of twig or grass stalk into the water. However, if you want to bring them in from any distance, or if you just want to show off a little, nothing beats fiddling.

The Ant Lion's Trap

The pitfall is a simple trap that has been brought to perfection by an insect called the ant lion. For millions of years, these ungainly creatures have constructed their cone-shaped pits and waited for some hapless insect to stray over the rim.

Yet, while these one- or two-inch pits are common throughout most of the United States, few people ever notice them. You don't have to go far to find these structures, but you do have to know where to look.

Ant lion traps are usually grouped together in loose, sandy soils, but don't be surprised if you find them in other materials as well. Over the years, people have reportedly found these tiny pits in rotted wood, gypsum, and even coal ashes. In selecting a site for its trap, the ant lion's primary consideration is that the soil (or material) must be free of vegetation and composed of small, dry, loosely packed particles. The insects also seem to require an overhang, such as a tree or the eaves of a building, which will shield their pits from the wind and rain. These two facts will help you locate any ant lions in your area.

It is actually the grotesque, half-inch larva of the ant lion that digs the pit. This larva, which begins life as an egg laid beneath the soil, starts to dig immediately after hatching, pushing itself backward and forcing the soil to slide over its back and onto its head. The insect then gives a quick flick of its head, and the soil is tossed up and out of the pit area. The larva continues this action, spiraling down in smaller and smaller circles, until it has created a cone-shaped depression in the soil that is usually about one or two inches deep.

Once its trap is constructed, the larva burrows into the soil near the bottom and waits. Sooner or later, some unsuspecting insect will step over the rim and onto the fine, sandy particles that make up the sides of the trap. These particles are so precariously balanced that the weight of the insect will trigger a miniature landslide that tumbles down the walls of the pit, alerting the ant lion to the presence of its prey.

As the ant lion's victim walks on the sloping sides of the pit, the loose soil falls away. The prey is now on a treadmill—moving its legs, yet going nowhere but down. Should the victim stop its descent, or make some progress in climbing up the trap walls, the ant lion springs into action and flicks its head, tossing soil at its prey. This rain of soil particles causes more of the trap's sides to tumble down and speeds the descent of the imperiled insect.

Once a trapped insect nears the bottom of the pit, the ant lion lunges forward and seizes it with its large, vicious-looking pincers. These pincers are larger than the ant lion's entire head, and inside them are tubes through which the ant lion injects a paralyzing fluid into the body of its prey. Later, after the ant lion has drained its prey of its body juices, it will throw the carcass up and out of the pit. Look around the outside of the trap and you are likely to see the remains of the ant lion's earlier meals. Ants make up the bulk of the ant lion's diet mainly because they are the most common wingless insects found in the ant lion's environment. However, spiders, beetles, sow bugs, caterpillars, and many other insects are consumed by this predator.

When you discover an ant lion's trap, take a small twig or a blade of grass and gently draw it along the sloping walls near the base of the pit. When this decoy gets within striking range, the hidden ant lion will make a lightning-fast flash of movement and grab for it. Immediately after this attack, the ant lion will retreat beneath the soil. If you look closely, you will still see those formidable jaws protruding just above the surface, ready to strike again.

If you would like to try something a little more theatrical, try bending down near an ant lion pit and calling to the hiding insects. Sometimes this will cause the ant lion to move and give away its position. It is unknown whether the ant lion moves because of vibrations set up by the sound of a voice or because of the air expelled from the mouth while speaking. Either way, this trick is impressive when it works.

Once you have seen the ant lion and its cone-shaped trap in action, you will understand why this insect is named for its ferocious larval stage rather than for the secretive, weak-flying adult, which looks much like a delicate damselfly. You will also wonder how you could have gone without noticing this mysterious and marvelous creature for so long.

Fiddling with Worms

Below the surface of every square mile of moist and fertile land, more than 32 million earthworms are moving about in over 20,000 miles of miniature tunnels.

Unless you're in deserts, high mountains, arctic regions, or areas with little soil or vegetation, you will always have several of these creatures or their tunnels directly underfoot when you stand outdoors.

Worms are easy to find, and they are always of interest because their ways seem so alien. But did you ever wonder how an animal with no arms or legs can make a tunnel? Most people have seen worms many times during their lives, yet few of them know that worms push themselves through cracks in the soil when it is soft, or eat their way through it if it is hard-packed. Using these simple methods of excavation, worms dig down as far as eight feet below the surface and can create an extensive complex of burrows in fewer than four days.

Another question that baffles most people is: What do worms eat? The answer is leaves and other plant debris found in and on the ground. One of our most common earthworms, the night crawler *(Lumbricus terrestris)*, creeps partway out of its burrow at night to grasp fallen leaves with its mouth and drag them back into its tunnel. Interestingly, these creatures always grab the pointy end of the leaf, the one that is most edible and easiest to slip into the hole. Then, having no teeth to chew with, the worm covers the leaf with saliva, which breaks it down until it is soft enough to be consumed. Often, the faint, rustling noise heard in woodlands and fields during spring and summer nights is the sound of night crawlers hauling leaves back into their holes.

When the night crawlers forage out of their holes, the time is ideal to do some worm hunting. To catch night crawlers, it is important to go to the right place at the right time. The best place is likely to be your own lawn, but any area covered with closely cropped grass will do just fine. The key factor is the moisture content of the soil. For the moister the soil, the closer the worms will be to its surface, thus increasing the likelihood that they will come out of their burrows. In fact, it is best to go worm hunting on a warm night after a long rain has thoroughly soaked the ground. Start looking for worms at least one hour after dark. By then, enough of them will have come to the surface to make the trip worthwhile.

Night crawlers do not simply lie around and wait to be picked up by the first human who strolls across the lawn. If you want to find worms, you have to be aware of a few basic rules. The first rule is to walk softly. Worms do not have ears, but they are very sensitive to vibrations passing through the ground. Have your companions put their hands flat on the ground while you step back several yards and stamp your feet. They will feel the vibrations each time your foot hits the ground and will quickly understand how worms "hear" and why everyone must refrain from galumphing across the lawn if they expect to capture any of these skittish creatures.

The second rule is to watch where the beam of your light is aimed. Night crawlers, as the name suggests, are creatures of darkness and they move upward out of their burrows as night approaches. They can detect different degrees of light, and they move toward dim light and away from bright light. This behavior is caused by certain photosensitive cells near the worm's head and is the source of an activity that can teach you something about how worms "see" the world around them.

To test a night crawler's reaction to light, make a small hole in a piece of paper or cloth and place it over the lens of a flashlight. This covering should leave enough diffused light to allow you to keep the worm in sight while creating a spot of bright light at the center of the beam. Move the bright spot along the body of the worm, starting at the point at which its tail disappears into its burrow; then move the beam up over the middle of the worm and onto its head. As the beam of light passes over the hind parts of the worm, you probably will not see any reaction at all. But when the bright light hits the head, the worm will jerk and pull back toward its hole. This reaction to the bright spot is the reason worm hunters never focus the beams of their lights directly on a worm, but keep it off to the side, using only the dim, peripheral light to illuminate a worm during their approach.

A worm's sense of touch is also concentrated near its head, and if you take a blade of grass and lightly touch a worm on the tail or at some point along its middle, it probably won't react very much. However, if you touch that same worm near the front of its body, it will immediately jerk itself backward. This variation in sensitivity between different parts of the same animal is much the same for human beings. To prove this, try the following experiment. First, pinch the skin on your elbow as hard as possible. The result will be very little or no pain, and you may marvel at how numb this part of the body is. Next, try to pinch the tops of your thighs as hard as you pinched your elbows. The reaction will definitely be very different, for the thigh area is rich in nerve endings and it hurts long before you can pinch it very hard.

When you have finally crept up on a night crawler and are about to pounce on it, the final rule of worm hunting comes into play. Never grab at a worm with your fingertips alone. Use your entire hand to grasp it, trying to capture it so that part of its head will protrude from the front of your hand. This technique is important because you can catch more worms this way, and you are less likely to injure them in the process.

Once the worm feels your hand, it will contract its body, wedge its tail into the burrow, and hang on for dear life. If you pull too hard, the worm will break in half before it lets go. To avoid this, lift the worm into a vertical position and pull gently. When the worm is taut, hold your hand steady and maintain the tension. Soon you will feel the worm let go and slide up into your hand. Another interesting way of getting worms out of their holes is to use your free hand to gently squeeze the head of a captured worm. Often, this squeeze is enough to induce a worm to release its hold on the burrow. Some people say this reaction occurs because the worm believes its head is safe inside another tunnel.

When you have caught a worm, run your fingers down its body, moving from the head toward the tail. As you do this, you will feel the rough bristles *(setae)* that the worm digs into the sides of its burrow when something tries to pull it out. These bristles also give the worm traction as it crawls through its tunnels or across the lawn. Don't be afraid to hold worms; worms can't bite, and they don't spread disease. Besides, to gain any real understanding of nature, you must learn to accept those parts of it that you may find alien or unappealing. These things, too, are a part of the ecological whole.

Worm hunts do not always take place under the cover of darkness, for there is a way to call worms out of their burrows in broad daylight. The technique has several different names, and depending on the region, it may be called worm-charming, grunting, or worm-fiddling. The last name is the one I grew up with, so it is the one I'll use.

Worm-fiddling is the art of generating vibrations beneath the surface of the soil to drive worms up from their tunnels. It is quite simple to perform, and all you need are two 18-inch wooden stakes. The stakes should be two or three inches wide, and one of them should have its end sharpened to a point. The unpointed stake should have notches cut along its length—notches deep enough to bump as it slides across the pointed stake, but not wide enough to catch on it.

When the stakes are ready, take them out to an area where the soil is moist (soak it the day before if necessary) and where wormholes are numerous and easily observed. When you find the right place, use a rock or hammer to pound the pointed stake about halfway into the ground. Next, begin pulling the notched edge of the free stake back and forth across the side of the one sunk in the ground, as if you were trying to saw through it. Immediately, you will feel the vibrations set up by this rasping of one stake against the other, and so will the worms.

If you have chosen the area well, worms should literally begin to ooze out of the ground within five or six minutes after you start fiddling. Children always marvel at this activity, but they are not the only ones who appreciate these minor miracles. The first time I tried worm-fiddling, I was working on the grounds crew at William Paterson College, and even my normally unflappable co-workers were impressed. For several days after I demonstrated this "trick," at least one of them would come up and say something like, "Hey, kid. Tell so-and-so how you call up worms."

This activity doesn't really require anything but worm-filled soil and a method of setting up vibrations. I have used steel rods and rocks instead of wooden stakes, and I have even seen people hold the butt end of a running chain saw on the trunk of a sapling to bring up worms. Anything will work well as long as the soil is moist and the worms are near the surface. If the soil is dry, the worms will be deeper and will take longer to get to the surface (if they come at all). But don't be discouraged. If you haven't seen any worms after 10 minutes of fiddling in one place, just move on.

Keep in mind that once a worm is taken from its burrow, it cannot find its way back again. So don't throw worms you have captured on the ground, leaving them to be eaten by predators or to dehydrate in the hot sun. Instead, cover them with grass and leaves, or direct the worm back to its hole. As you watch a worm crawl back down into the earth, think about what it would be like to live underground, in a place where grass roots hang down from above and the thunder of giant footsteps is always rumbling overhead. It is an interesting change in perspective—one that will make you a little more conscious of what goes on in the soil beneath your feet.

The Wonder of Webs

$\mathcal{A}$ morning dew is the tattletale of the spider world. Highlighting every web with a veneer of tiny droplets, it exposes them to our view and makes us aware of how many spiders are around us.

Look at any dew-covered field and you will surely see dozens of webs glistening in the grass and among the branches of any brush in the area. Yet there are many more spiders than webs in that field, and some studies have shown that up to two million of them may live on a single acre of field or meadow. Most of these spiders are secretive and will spend their lives hidden from our view, but a few of them are quite easy to find, and these can be the focus of some intriguing activities.

The most familiar of all spiderwebs are the large, symmetrical nets of the orb weavers. You can find these webs, often measuring more than a foot in diameter, in fields, gardens, woodlands, and just about any place else the spiders can find to work their craft. I have even found one of these structures built between the rearview mirror and dashboard of my car, for when spiders search for a place to build webs, there seems to be no limit to their ingenuity.

Orb weavers all have rather poor vision and sense the world mainly through vibrations in their webs. Depending on the species, they either wait motionless in the center of their orbs or lurk in some well-hidden spot off to one side. But no matter where these spiders wait, their legs are always touching the web, alert for the disturbance that occurs when anything blunders into their traps.

You can usually find the spider's hideout by following its trail of web to a rolled-up leaf or a crevice in a wall. However, some of these creatures are masters of concealment, and there have been times when I have looked directly at an inch-long garden spider *(Araneus diadematus)* and not even realized it was there. How can you get one of these hidden spiders to reveal its position? It's easy. Set up vibrations that will trick the spider into thinking something has been caught in its web.

The keys to success in this endeavor are a light touch and a slender probe. Pick up a thin blade of grass or a leaf stem and gently touch it to one of the circular threads that make up the spiral part of the web. When the tip of the probe contacts the web, roll the probe rapidly back and forth between your fingers. Roll it five or six times and rest for two seconds. Then roll it several more times. If you act quickly and delicately, you will create vibrations similar to those made by a captured insect that is frantically trying to free itself from the web. Suddenly, with a burst of speed that can be startling, the spider will rush forth from its hiding place and dash across the web toward your decoy. Be sure to probe the web as gently as possible. If you use a heavy hand, the spider will remain in hiding or drop to the ground and run off into the grass, afraid of the giant that is jiggling its home.

This web-shaking technique works only about 50 percent of the time, but when it does work, you will be in for a thrill. There is something about our combined fascination and fear of spiders that makes interacting with them especially exciting. Use this activity to make children feel a bit more comfortable around these marvelous creatures. The more children get to know spiders, the more they will accept them as a normal part of their everyday environment.

Whereas most orb weavers live outdoors, other spiders have taken up residence inside our buildings. The long-bodied cellar spider *(Pholcus phalungioides)* is one of those that live indoors, and you can find it in basements, attics, and garages throughout the United States. Look for these gangly creatures in an out-of-the-way part of your house. You can usually find them hanging upside down in their loose, cobweblike webs in dimly lit areas.

The long-bodied cellar spider is tan-colored and about one-quarter inch long, although this creature is named for the length of its body, the length of its legs is really its most noticeable feature. These legs can be up to two inches long and make this spider look like a daddy long-legs with a web. When you locate one of these spiders, blow several puffs of air at it. The spider and its web will lurch as the air hits it, and after it has been buffeted several times, the spider will either walk away or perform one of the most astonishing feats ever seen: it will disappear right before your eyes.

The spider accomplishes this vanishing act by clinging to its web and flexing its muscles, which starts the spider's body swinging in a circular pattern. The first few swings will be slow enough for your eyes to follow, but once the spider builds up speed, all that can be seen is a blur. If the light is dim, the spider will seem to disappear completely. You know it is there, but you can't see it. This trick is something of an illusion and is unique, for no other common, North American animal utilizes this form of defense.

Often the same spider can be prompted to do its trick a second time, but when it tires of this game, it will walk off the web and climb onto the wall. Leave it alone, and it will eventually go back to its web, ready to vanish again at your command sometime in the future.

People usually have difficulty believing that spiders sometimes fly. "How can they fly if they don't have wings?" they ask. Actually, spiders don't really fly, but they do glide through the air on long strands of web. This type of flight is called *ballooning*, and by using this method of dispersal, spiders have been sighted landing on a ship 200 miles away from the nearest land and have been collected while floating at altitudes of 16,000 feet (over 3 miles straight up). It is even possible that spiders have crossed the Atlantic Ocean riding these long filaments of web. Of course, a spider cannot steer itself while ballooning, but since most spiders use this technique to travel short distances at low altitudes, steering isn't important.

Spiders have two methods of taking off. They either release strands of silk into the wind until the strands are long enough to carry them aloft; or they hang down on a line from some elevated object, releasing web and lowering themselves into the breeze until the line breaks and they are airborne. This second method of takeoff provides us with an opportunity to watch spiders glide from our hands.

On a breezy day, catch a small spider on a stick, hold the stick at shoulder level, and tap it with your finger. The jolt of the tap will cause the spider to fall and dangle from the stick on a long thread of web. Keep the spider in this position, but don't let it drop all the way to the ground, or it will run off and escape. If the spider climbs back up to the stick, tap it again. The goal is to keep the spider dangling in midair.

Once the spider is hanging down from the stick, turn your body so the full force of the breeze can hit the spider. If you are lucky, the spider will begin to release more strands of silk as the moving air jostles it. When these strands are long enough, the spider will break free of the line connected to your hand and will float away on the breeze.

This ballooning activity works best with crab spiders and with the spiderlings of many other species. As soon as the spider is airborne, follow after it. Ballooning spiders soar erratically, much like soap bubbles in a current of air; and children always find great pleasure in this chase, following the floating spider until the breeze lifts it high into the sky or carries it over some obstacle that ends their pursuit.

The Miracle of a Monarch

Although you must be out-of-doors to witness most natural wonders, there is one natural miracle you can observe in the comfort of your home. You don't need much in the way of equipment or time.

In fact, all you need is a large jar or aquarium and the time to look for a colorful caterpillar that you will find feeding on the local milkweed plants.

The caterpillar you are looking for is the larval stage of the orange-and-black monarch butterfly *(Danaus plexippus)*, and two things about these insects make them easy to find. First, the female monarch lays its eggs only on milkweed plants, and the emergent caterpillars will eat nothing else. If you can locate a stand of milkweed, you have found the primary habitat of your quarry. Second, the monarch caterpillar is quite large and colored with a series of alternating black, white, and yellow bands, making it hard to overlook. These gaudy caterpillars are truly conspicuous and make no attempt to hide themselves. In fact, you can often find them stretched out across the top of a leaf in full view.

When you find one of these brightly colored caterpillars, you will probably wonder why this species is so showy, while most other species blend in with their surroundings to avoid becoming the dinner of some hungry bird. The answer is that the monarch caterpillar's bright colors are a warning of danger to birds. This warning is no bluff because the leaves of the milkweed plant, which make up the entire diet of the monarch, are filled with chemicals that are absorbed into the caterpillar's body as it digests the leaves. These chemicals—called *cardiac glycosides,* for those who prefer scientific terminology—are quite potent and will make any bird that eats a monarch caterpillar violently ill, teaching it to avoid all caterpillars colored with black, white, and yellow bands.

Another question you might ask is which end of the caterpillar is the head. Silly as this question seems, the answer is not always clear at first glance, since both ends of monarch caterpillars look much the same. To solve this riddle, examine the caterpillar closely and you will notice that the antennae on one end of the caterpillar are larger than those on the other end. These longer antennae are on the caterpillar's head. The purpose of these similar-looking ends is to mislead predators into attacking the less vital tail area, giving the caterpillar a greater chance of escaping with only nonlethal wounds if it is attacked.

After you have observed the caterpillar in its natural surroundings, pick it up and gently place it in a container along with some fresh milkweed leaves. Next, collect several short, well-leafed stalks of milk-weed and head for home. You have just acquired a pet that will soon change from a bulky, crawling leaf eater into a dainty, flying creature that feeds only on the sweet nectar of flowers. No one knows exactly how this transformation is accomplished, but there is a name for the process. We call it *metamorphosis,* and while it is a common occurrence among insects, none do it as beautifully as the monarch.

When you get home, find a large, clear container for your caterpillar—aquariums, big fishbowls, and large, widemouthed glass jars are all suitable. Next, fill a small, narrow-necked jar with water, cover its opening with a piece of aluminum foil or cloth, and push the stem of a milkweed stalk through this cover and down into the water. Then, set the small bottle in the center of the large container, place your caterpillar on the milkweed, and cover the opening of the large container with a piece of screen, nylon mesh, cheesecloth, or anything else that will prevent the caterpillar from climbing out while allowing air to flow in. As long as the milkweed is in the water, the plant will continue to live and provide food for the caterpillar. The cover over the water container is there to prevent the caterpillar from climbing down the stalk and drowning.

Once you have your caterpillar ensconced in its new home, you have little more to do except add fresh milkweed when needed, clean out the jar every few days, and watch your caterpillar eat and grow. Remember to place the container in a location that is not exposed to the direct rays of the sun, which might raise the temperature inside to a point that is fatal to the caterpillar.

Your caterpillar will begin to feed almost as soon as it is placed upon the milkweed plant you have provided. Look closely and you will see that its mouth closes from side to side—rather than top to bottom—which is quite handy for a creature that feeds on the edges of leaves. Day after day, the caterpillar will chew semicircular holes into the leaf margins and grow at a tremendous rate. The caterpillar's main task in life is to convert plant tissue into caterpillar bulk, and it does this so effectively that if a 9-pound human baby grew as fast as a newborn caterpillar, it would weigh 20 tons by the time it was two weeks old.

The caterpillar will eat constantly until it is ready to shed its skin or pupate. When it reaches one of these junctures in its development, it will stop eating for a day or so and remain motionless, sometimes abandoning the food plant to wander about or rest on the side of the container. This resting phase takes place before the next stage of growth begins, for inside the caterpillar's body, complex chemical processes are forming a new skin beneath the one you see.

After the resting period, the caterpillar spins a small button of silk, which it grips with its rear claspers while the rest of its body hangs head downward. Once in this position, the caterpillar begins to contort its body and swing back and forth in an effort to detach the old skin from the new one that has grown beneath it. As the two skins separate, the old outer skin loses much of its color and becomes noticeably rumpled. Next, a split appears just behind the head, and the old skin is forced back upward and finally discarded. Since the caterpillar is dangling from a thin pad of silk that, if damaged, would make it difficult for the caterpillar to climb out of its old skin, your caterpillar must be left undisturbed during the process of molting.

A monarch caterpillar sheds its skin four times and grows larger between each molt. When the old skin has been shed, the caterpillar remains hanging quietly while the new skin hardens. The first three molts result in a larger caterpillar with brighter-looking colors and baggy, wrinkled skin that will fill out when the larva gets back to serious eating. The fourth molt, which will happen within four weeks of the date you acquire the caterpillar, ends with something far more mysterious and beautiful: a pupa contained in jade green chrysalis flecked with dots of gold.

As during the other molts, the caterpillar will stop feeding and become quiet when it is ready to pupate. However, after this period of quiescence, the caterpillar will begin to roam around, leaving the milkweed plant to look for an elevated place from which to suspend itself. It must find a place where it can hang freely, for if it touches anything while the chrysalis is forming or upon emerging when its wings are soft, deformity or death could quite possibly result. Thus the cover on the caterpillar's container should be made of cheesecloth, some sort of mesh, or other material to which the caterpillar can easily cling. If for some reason you prefer not to use the mesh, brace a twig high up against the side of the container so it forms a wide angle with several inches of its surface at least six inches above the bottom. Either one of these methods will allow the caterpillar to get into the proper position to pupate.

When the caterpillar finds the right spot, it will begin to sway back and forth, laying down a button of silk on the supporting object. Next, it will grasp the silk with its rear claspers and hang in an inverted J-shaped position formed by curving its head inward toward its body. This entire procedure may take the better part of a day.

In time, a split will appear in the skin behind the head, and the caterpillar will begin to wriggle violently, attempting to shed its larval skin for the last time. As the skin splits and moves away from the head, a large drop of thick, green liquid will appear. When the old skin is finally shed, this green material will harden into the emerald-colored case that protects the pupa as it undergoes its transformation into a butterfly. For the next 9 to 15 days, much of what was previously a caterpillar changes to liquid and rearranges itself into an adult butterfly. How this happens is still a mystery, and the entire transformation takes place without causing the chrysalis to so much as twitch.

As time passes, the chrysalis changes from green to teal blue to brown and eventually becomes transparent, allowing the orange-and-black wings of the adult butterfly to show through. If you look closely, you will see the black body of the butterfly hanging head downward, awaiting the right moment to break free. Finally, a split forms at the bottom of the chrysalis, and the new butterfly climbs awkwardly out and clings to its old chrysalis. Leave your pet alone during this transformation. When a butterfly first emerges, its wings are folded and limp, and it must hang downward while they are pumped up with body fluid. If anything jars the butterfly, it may fall from its perch to the ground, where its wings will become deformed. If, for some very good reason, you must move the butterfly, try prompting it to cling to your finger or some other object and transfer it that way.

Although the wing-pumping process takes about 20 minutes, the wings will not be hard enough to endure flight for another hour or so. Once the butterfly is able to fly, you should set your pet free. Bring the container outside, open the top, and place it where the butterfly can easily fly away. If the butterfly clings to the mesh cover, lift the entire cover up and hang it outdoors. Never touch the wings of your butterfly because they are very fragile and easily damaged. Again, if you must remove the butterfly from the jar, coax it onto your finger, a twig, or some other object that will let your pet support its weight on its legs.

Watching the butterfly you raised flap its wings and become airborne for the first time is a marvelous experience. For the first several days after leaving, the butterfly will feed heavily on the flowers in your area. It no longer has the side-closing mouth so well suited for chewing leaves; instead, its mouth is a long tube that it uses like a drinking straw to draw liquid nectar up from deep inside flowers. If your butterfly emerges early in the summer, it will travel north and continue to reproduce along the way. If it is late in the season, your butterfly will head south to Mexico (if you found it east of the Rocky Mountains) or California (if you found it west of the Rocky Mountains), where it will winter in protected groves with millions of others of its kind.

This annual migration of monarchs is unique among butterflies and can be the inspiration for children to take an imaginary journey. Migrating monarchs fly only during the day, traveling at about the same speed as a jogger moving at a quick pace. With a favorable wind, these creatures can cover up to 80 miles in a single day, but the average distance they travel in that time is slightly less than 40 miles.

If you estimate that your butterfly is traveling at 35 miles a day, you can follow its possible progress on a map. Easterners should plot a line from their location south or southwest to the region of central Mexico. If this course brings your butterfly to the Gulf of Mexico, plot its course to the Gulf Coast and then west along the shoreline until it can follow a southwestern route overland to the center of Mexico. Those living in the western United States should plot a line from their homes to the area around the California towns of Santa Cruz or Pacific Grove. Every evening before bedtime, sit down with your children and plot on a map the possible location of their butterfly. If you can get a good atlas with details of the physical geography and description of the region the butterfly is crossing, you can make up tales of flights over mountains, cornfields, and county fairs. Every 3 days, your butterfly will cover about 100 miles, and it will travel 8 to 10 weeks before it reaches Mexico from the northern sections of its range.

If you did not raise a butterfly from a caterpillar, but would still like to take an imaginary trip with a monarch, simply go outdoors during the early days of autumn and look for a monarch butterfly as it flutters by. Take a compass along and you will notice that the great majority of the monarchs that you see are heading south or southwest. Explain to the children that this special butterfly migrates like a bird and heads south for the winter. Then let the tales of the great journey begin. The migration story is a good way to teach geography, and you can use it as a special bedtime activity that only you and the children will share.

Bee Hunting

Honeybees have always known that the shortest distance between two points is a straight line. A bee may zigzag as it travels from blossom to blossom, but as soon as it gathers a full load of nectar, it will fly back to the hive in as direct a route as the terrain allows—a route we have come to know as a beeline.

A bee can plot a direct course to its hive because it navigates by the sun, but even more fascinating is the fact that this same bee can communicate directions to its fellow workers, instructing them how to retrace the route back to a food source. Soon after learning the location of the nectar-rich flowers, a steady flow of bees will be moving both ways along a beeline between them and the hive. This creates an aerial trail you can follow if you are attentive and patient.

Old-timers in the southern hills called the art of following bees *coursin'*, and most of the bee-tracking skills they learned as children remain essentially unchanged. The first step in tracking bees is to locate some foraging bees or bring them to the bee hunter's location. In the old days, bee hunters heated large, flat rocks in an open fire and removed them when they were scalding hot. Next, they placed a piece of honeycomb on the hot rock, which melted the wax and filled the air with the sweet fragrance of honey—an aroma honeybees find irresistible.

Soon the rock was swarming with bees gathering up the honey, and the bee hunter would follow the beeline back to the hive unless he or she lost the trail. At this point, the bee hunter would build another fire and begin all over again, knowing that any bees passing by on their way back to the first site would catch the scent of the new bait and be lured to it. This method of bee hunting took a lot of work, but in earlier times when sugar or sweets of any kind were rare, the hunt for honey was well worth the effort.

Today, instead of using a campfire and hot rocks, you may want to try a modern method. First, light a wide, unscented candle (preferably one made of beeswax) and wait until the flame has caused a small pool of melted wax to collect at the base of the wick. When the pool has formed, pour a small amount of honey onto the melted wax. The wax will heat the honey and send its sweet scent wafting off to entice some foraging bee.

If this candle method seems unsafe or inconvenient, you can use a scent post to lure bees. A scent post is a piece of cloth or a leafy twig that has been sprinkled with a fragrant substance and, if necessary, set upon a stick or branch to keep it above the ground. Again, the idea is to use the bee's keen sense of smell to lure it to your position. Long tradition and my own experience hold that anise oil is one of the best all-around bee lures that is readily available. This clear oil is found in the spice aisle of most supermarkets and has a strong licorice odor that bees find attractive.

When the scent has done its work and lured a bee to your position, an abundant source of food should be nearby. This food is the bait that will bring the bee back with its fellow workers. What ambrosia will entice a bee to begin feeding? All you need is a mixture made of equal parts of sugar and water or a small amount of honey. Place either of these substances in a shallow dish with stones or twigs for the bees to stand on while feeding, and wait for your "guide" bee to drink its fill.

Once the first bee has revealed the location of your bait, other workers will swarm out of the hive to gather up this bonanza. Within 30 or 40 minutes, there will be a dozen or so bees working the bait, and the route these bees travel as they fly to and from the hive will be straight and sure: a beeline. Now the hunt begins as you try to follow these bees on their return trip to the hive, but like all trades, bee hunting has certain tricks that can make the difference between success and failure.

The most important technique beginners need to learn is to place the bait in an open area where the bees are in full view as they arrive and depart. Bees usually lift off the bait and circle around in the air several times before they find the direction leading straight to the hive. If the area isn't clear, you will lose sight of them before figuring out which way they went.

Once you have identified the beeline, make a mental note of some landmark the bees pass over as they fly back to the hive and walk over to it. Then, keeping in sight the next several bees that pass over this new position, pinpoint another landmark farther down the beeline and move to it. Continue this leapfrogging procedure as long as you can.

If you lose track of the bees, walk 50 or 100 yards in the direction they were traveling and set up a new scent post and bait dish. Some of the bees heading toward your first scent post will surely be lured to the new bait and will lead the others to it. Soon you should be able to close up the first bait dish and pick up the trail again as the bees move back and forth between your new bait and their hive. Repeat this procedure as often as necessary, and eventually you will find yourself at the entrance to their hive.

Remember that a beeline is never exactly straight. Overall, the route bees take in both directions will be straight, but one bee may swerve to the left to avoid an obstacle while another veers to the right or climbs into the sky and flies over it. Despite these minor deviations from course, the hive will be within 20 degrees of the beeline being followed. In addition, keep in mind that bees rarely forage beyond two miles from the hive. If the bees do not come to your new bait in about 20 minutes, go back to the last location the bees came to and set up again. You may have passed the hive or wandered too far from the beeline.

The beehive will most likely be in the rotten core of a living deciduous tree with a trunk two feet or more in diameter. Honeybees do not seem to favor any one species of tree, and I have found hives in oaks and maples as well as in willows and poplars. The entrance hole can be anywhere along the trunk of the tree, but no matter where it is, if the bees are working a food source, there will be a continuous stream of them moving in and out of the tree or hovering in front of the entrance waiting to get inside.

Although you can bait bees throughout the warmer parts of the year, the best time to hunt them is in the early spring when the temperature first begins to reach 50°F. At this time of the year, bees are "winter hungry" and the hive's honey reserves are at their lowest. The bees are ready to feed, and there are few flowers around to compete with the bait you are offering. Also, the trees are still leafless, so you are less likely to lose track of a bee in the foliage.

Should you discover bees close to home, you can train them to come for a "visit" at the same time each day. To get them started, put out a scent post and bait every day at the same time and place, and remove it about one hour later. After feeding on schedule for about a week, the bees will start coming to the baited area only during the time they are accustomed to getting food; you can almost set your watch by their arrival. It's fun to set up this feeding station in advance and tell your friends that you have scheduled a luncheon with some bees. The looks on their faces when your "guests" begin to arrive are priceless.

Honeybees are able to arrive on time for their visits because they have an internal clock that is attuned to the 24-hour solar day—an attribute valuable to creatures that navigate by the sun and must arrive at plants during the hours when nectar flow is fullest. Once you have trained the bees, follow them until you find the hidden place where they live. If you are within two miles of an apiary, you may find that the bees belong to a neighbor. Even so, tracking these tiny creatures to their lair is an accomplishment you can be proud of and a small adventure you will enjoy.

Playing
with Plants

Grasping Grapes

Over four and one-half centuries before Christopher Columbus was even born, a Viking ship cruised the waters off New England. The old Norse sagas say the crew of this ship went ashore and named the place Vinland (Wineland) after the abundant wild grapes they found growing there.

Although no one has ever been able to locate precisely where this historic landing took place, it is still easy to find the wild grapes that inspired those early explorers.

Wild grapes grow in the thickets and open woodlands of the eastern United States. The fruit is not especially good for eating because it is usually too tart. However, although the fruit may not appeal to humans, it definitely appeals to wildlife. Over 80 species of birds eat the fruit in its season, and box turtles, black bears, rabbits, raccoons, and many other common animals join them in this feast. White-tailed deer browse the grapevine itself, and many birds use the peeling bark of the woody vine to build their nests. In fact, I've never found a cardinal's nest without at least a few strands of wild grape bark woven into it.

Grapevines are always hungry for sunlight and will climb any tree or shrub within reach. Their climbing is accomplished by tendrils: thin, usually forked, stemlike structures that grow opposite the leaves. These tendrils are soft and weak until they make contact with something; then they begin a remarkable transformation. First, they coil around and around whatever they have touched; and later, when they have finished coiling, they begin to thicken and become woody, preparing to act as supports that will allow the vine to climb even higher.

A grapevine tendril's response to touch, called *thigmotropism,* is the source of an activity that can be enjoyed by anyone who can still find excitement in nature's small wonders. When you come upon a grapevine, look around for a thick blade of grass or a leaf stem and tie it in a loop. Next, set the loop over the end of a grapevine's tendril and leave it dangling there. Since this is not one of those activities that provides immediate feedback, continue on with your business, and return to the grapevine after an hour or so. When you come back, you will find that the previously straight tendril has already begun to coil itself around your loop. Return again a day later, and your loop will be thoroughly secured with coil after coil of tightly wound tendril; it will look as if a botanical boa constrictor has seized it. This little stunt never fails and illustrates the fact that plants can "feel" and move in response to their environment.

Raising
a Ruckus

Somehow, an unwritten law
has evolved that requires people
always to remain silent upon
entering the woods or while
crossing a meadow. I don't know
how such a rigid rule ever got
started, but I believe that there is
a time and place for everything—
a time for silence and a time to
make some noise.

The serious wildlife watcher will want to muffle his or her footsteps and not even speak in whispers, but people afield with a child or two can probably have a better day out if they just let the kids follow their own lead, and maybe even encourage them a bit. Little children love to make big noises, and even adults are not beyond the thrill of this activity—especially if they feel that they can relax and not appear to be foolish.

The easiest way to generate an amusing clamor is to make grass whistles. Pick a blade of grass around one-half inch wide and lay it on the outside edge of one of your thumbs. Next, place the outside edge of your other thumb on the opposite side of the grass, keeping it taut and tightly sandwiched between the two thumbs. Keeping the blade of grass in place, bring your thumbs up so that they are vertical and blow into the gap that naturally forms between them. As you do this, the air will pass through the gap and around the taut blade of grass, making a shrill sound that will startle anyone trying this whistle for the first time. Actually, the sound produced is not a clear whistle at all, and this instrument would be better named a grass yowler instead of a grass whistle. However, I am not one to break with the traditions of my playground days.

An acorn cap whistle is another noisemaker that is fun to try out if you are in the vicinity of an oak tree. These whistles are not as easy to use as grass whistles, but if you want to show off a little, it's worth the effort to learn. Begin by placing your thumbs across the hollow side of an acorn cap, positioning them so they are just a little short of completely covering its upper edge. This will leave a small, V-shaped opening above your thumbs. Blow into the base of this V, and you will soon hear a sound like that of a greatly amplified whistling teakettle. It's fun to try this with several different types of acorn caps because each cap has unique acoustical properties that affect the pitch of the whistle. For those of you who can't manage to get to an oak tree, try a bottle cap instead. These caps lack the natural appeal of acorn caps, but they are readily available and work quite well.

Although whistles are fun, no sound can rival an explosive *bang* for getting people's attention. Think about it: fireworks, gunshots, backfires, and the slam of a teacher's ruler on a desk can all make us perk up and listen. There is just something about these sounds that always catches us by surprise, and a simple device I call the "leaf whacker" will let you make a surprising *pop* anytime you wish.

The main ingredient for making one of these noisemakers is a broad leaf with no holes in it (maple or grape leaves work well). After you find one, make a ring with the index finger and thumb of one hand, and place the leaf so it completely covers this ring. When the leaf is in position, strike it hard with the open palm of your hand. If you do it right, you will get a loud *pop* as the air compressed by your hand bursts through the leaf. Do this unexpectedly and all eyes, human and wild, will be on you. But remember that this activity is contagious, and once you get some people started, it may be difficult to get them to stop. Don't let these folks strip too many leaves from one plant though; nature has other plans for them.

Plants to Wear

People have always worn the flowers and foliage of plants. They put blossoms in their hair and buttonholes for decoration; they arrange twigs and brush on their clothing as camouflage; and, in some tropical areas, they wear large leaves on their heads as makeshift hats.

This botanical costuming is a thoroughly human trait—one that is certainly acceptable to children, who always seem eager to do a little "dressing up."

During spring, when dandelions are in rampant bloom across much of America, younger children can find great pleasure in making dandelion chains. Begin by plucking several dandelions from the ground, taking care to harvest as much of the stem as possible. Next, remove the flower heads from the stems and insert the smaller end of the hollow stem into the larger one, creating a circle. Run the next stem through this circle and repeat the process of joining the ends together. If the children want to create necklaces, run the last stem through the two end links of the chain and join them together. These dandelion chains are very easy to make and are strong enough to be constructed to absurd lengths. After the novelty of wearing the chains as necklaces has worn off, have the children join all the smaller chains together to create one long chain. As always, when it's a matter of "bigger is better," kids can be expected to rise to the challenge.

As spring gives way to summer, and the flowers of the open fields begin to bloom, we have the opportunity to fashion what has to be the most romantic of all quick-and-easy floral creations: the crown of daisies. To make one, pick a handful of daisies, leaving two or three inches of stem attached to each blossom. After gathering the flowers, use your fingernail to make a small slit in one of the stems about a half inch below the blossom, and then thread the stem of a second flower through this slit. Pull the second stem down until the flower head is butted up against the first stem, make a slit in the second stem, and thread a third flower stem through it. Continue this process until the crown is the right size for the recipient's head. To complete the crown, make a larger slit in the last stem, and carefully lift the blossom of the first flower through it.

The daisy crown does not really have to be made of daisies; in fact, these garlands need not even be crowns, but can be worn as necklaces, bracelets, or even belts. I have made them from Queen Anne's lace, coneflowers, goldenrod, asters, and just about every other common flower with a reasonably thick, firm stem. Everyone appreciates these bright creations, and when you set one upon somebody's head—child or adult—you give a gift that is somehow far more significant than the materials used to form it would ever suggest.

The fallen leaves of autumn provide the opportunity to make leaf crowns, a dress-up activity that even preteen boys—who would never wear a garland of flowers on their heads—will enjoy. Look for a tree that has shed wide, colorful leaves, and gather a dozen or so of the very best specimens into a small pile. One by one, break the stems off these leaves and heap them together. Next, take two of the stemless leaves and lay one on top of the other so that they partially overlap. Now, pin these leaves together by pushing one of the stems down through the overlapping section and up again a short distance away. Continue to attach the leaves together in this manner, and when the string of leaves is long enough to fit snugly around the child's brow, pin the first and last leaves together.

The leaves you put together do not have to be worn only on the head. They can be worn as belts, necklaces, or even a vest if one has the patience to make it. Since maple leaves are large, well-shaped, and colorful, they are the perennial favorites of crown makers. But I have also had excellent results with large hickory, oak, and sweet gum leaves. The type of leaf you use really doesn't matter very much, as long as it is large and firm enough to hold together when a stem is run through it.

If you have found a nearby maple to build crowns with, remember it during spring when it begins to drop its seeds. When no one is looking, break one of the mustache-shaped pods in half, split the seed end with your fingernail, and press the moist, sticky interior of the seed to the tip of your nose. Spin around and tell the children you have the nose and strength of a rhinoceros and that you want everyone to look just like you. In no time at all, the children will have maple-seed tusks on their noses, and soon they will put them on their earlobes, foreheads, fingertips, and anyplace else they can get them to stick. This activity may not be very educational, but it is a surefire way to put everyone in a playful mood.

.

.

.

The Age of Pines

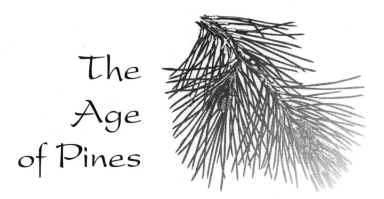

Walk into a pine grove, and you immediately understand why the ancients felt awed by these places. Pine groves are always darker than other parts of the woods, and they are mysteriously quiet. Even your footsteps are muffled by the fallen needles that carpet the area.

In many cultures, these evergreens have been regarded as symbols of eternal life. Yet, ironically, these are the very trees that most readily reveal their age.

Pine trees look as if they are made up of layers of branches with the widest layers on the bottom and the narrowest on top. This layered structure forms because, every year, each pine grows one central bud surrounded by a ring of lateral buds at the very top of its trunk. In the spring, the central bud will grow straight upward while the lateral buds will grow out sideways, forming a new layer of branches in a ring around the trunk. Each layer of branches, called a *whorl* by botanists, equals one year of growth. It you count the number of layers on a pine tree, and add four to account for its seedling years, you will know the approximate age of the tree.

If you want to know how tall the tree was when you were born, just count down your age in layers from the top. If you are with a young child, this activity is especially meaningful because children don't really have a good idea of what 20, 30, and 40 years can mean; they haven't lived that long yet. But when you demonstrate that a tall pine was just a sprout when you were born, they will view time with different eyes. Suddenly, you are not just old; you are venerable.

Older pines tend to lose their lower branches. To age these trees you will have to go up close and count the scars on the trunk that were left when the branches fell off. The layer-counting technique works well in aging the local pine and spruce species, but it doesn't work with all evergreens. Look for the layers (whorls) of branches before you start.

If the temperature is below freezing, you can do one more thing with evergreen trees—especially an old Christmas tree. After all the ornaments and lights have been removed, take the tree outside and set it up near an outdoor faucet. Next, get out the garden hose and spray nozzle you put away in the fall. Tie the nozzle near the top of the tree and set it so it will send a fine, misty spray straight up into the air. Attach the hose and turn on the water. The mist will shoot straight up and fall gently down, covering your tree with tiny water droplets that will quickly turn to ice. In no time at all, your tree will be covered with a coat of pure crystal.

Don't leave the water on too long, unless you want icicles, and be sure to drain the hose and faucet before they freeze. If the weather stays cold, your dazzling crystal tree will last for days. Try this activity once, and you may find that it becomes an annual event.

Jewelweed Explosions & the Mountain Laurel's Catapult

If nature ran a novelty shop, it would always keep a large supply of jewelweed *(Impatiens capensis)* in stock. It would have to; children would demand it. For these common woodland plants have the surprising ability to startle a human audience and keep them coming back for more.

Fortunately, you do not have to go to a curio shop to find jewelweed. Just walk along the bank of any stream or into a moist, wooded area, and you will probably find this plant growing in such lush abundance that it will seem to have a monopoly there. Once you find some, call everyone over. It is time for some wizardry.

Jewelweed is a light-green plant that grows from two to five feet tall, and it doesn't seem to be anything special until you pluck one of its lance-shaped leaves and hold it under water. Suddenly, your plain, green leaf will look as if it is covered with a film of the most richly polished silver. This film appears to be magic, but it is actually a natural form of waterproofing. The silvery sheen is caused by a thin layer of air that is trapped on the surface of the leaf and reflects the light of the sun. Lift the leaf out of the water and it is miraculously dry. This is one of those activities that make great props for tales about alchemists, sorcery, and enchanted forests.

The real magic of the jewelweed does not develop until late in the summer, well after the plant has colored its habitat with a profusion of spurred, orange or yellow blossoms. Jewelweed flowers hang down in pairs by thin, threadlike stalks and are visited by hordes of hungry bees that energetically buzz from one blossom to the next gathering nectar and spreading pollen. When the flowers have been fertilized and the seed has set, the jewelweed blossoms begin to transform themselves into one of the trailside's most captivating amusements: exploding seedpods.

Look for these swollen, cigar-shaped pods in the late summer or early fall. When you find them, pinch the bottom tip of a big, fat one. Before you can bring any real pressure to bear on it, the pod will explode, triggered by your touch. Sometimes you can actually hear the pod shoot its seeds out, propelling them up to six feet away.

After you have exploded one of these pods, take another look at it. What was a cigar-shaped seed container a moment ago is now a twisted tangle of fiber. This explosive performance gives the jewelweed its other common name: touch-me-not.

When you have finished "popping" the individual pods, take a stick and gently thrash it around in the center of the touch-me-not grove. By doing this, you will explode hundreds of pods at once as the plants jostle against one another. All those seeds flying around will look like a giant, out-of-control popcorn machine, and it's enough to make children watching this wild event absolutely giggly.

Another plant with a hair trigger is the mountain laurel *(Kalmia latifolia)*, a shrub whose leathery green leaves resemble those of a rhododendron. However, unlike jewelweed, the most interesting part of this plant is its flowers, and each year during the spring and early summer, its clusters of white or pinkish blossoms offer an intriguing little diversion that is nothing short of delightful.

The individual flower of the mountain laurel is cup-shaped with 10 stringy stamens rising up from its center. Unlike those of other plants, these stamens do not stick straight up in the air. Instead, they are bent back like drawn bows, and the knobs at the end of each filament, called *anthers,* are each held in a tiny pocket just below the area where the petals begin to turn upward.

Each stamen is like a miniature catapult that is cocked back and ready to fire. When a hungry bee comes to sip the nectar at the center of the flower, it cannot avoid bumping into one or more of these bent filaments. As this happens, the knobby anther is pulled from its pocket and springs upward, shooting its pollen onto the back of the bee.

If you pass a mountain laurel when it is in bloom, stop and set off its catapults by using a twig to nudge the arching filaments of the stamens. As soon as one is touched, the stamen will whip up toward the center of the flower. If you watch closely, you may even see the small dab of yellowish-white pollen shoot out from the anther.

Exploding jewelweed pods and setting off mountain laurel flowers are captivating pastimes, so if you are in a hurry to get somewhere, don't point out these activities to any children you may have along. If you do, you will have a hard time getting the kids moving again. These activities are custom-made for dawdlers.

Experiencing Earth, Sea, & Sky

High Adventure Close to the Ground

*C*hildren see an invitation to climb written on the rocky face of every cliff. They can hardly resist the offer, and the moment they are in the presence of some minor Matterhorn, they begin scrambling up the rock, eager to meet the challenges of the ascent.

Parents read cliffs with different eyes. For them, the word *danger* seems to be the only message written on the rock. Thus the stage is set for one of the classic bottom-of-the-cliff, parent-child conversations. "Come down from there." "Do I have to?" "Yes." "Why?" "It's dangerous." "I'll be careful." "I said, no!" "Please." "I said, no!!"

Exchanges such as this one never turn out well; the children end up feeling frustrated while their parents guiltily wonder if they have been overprotective. Fortunately, the sport of bouldering is an alternative that allows children to experience the thrill of climbing while remaining at a height acceptable to worried parents. This sport is simple, safe, fun, and teaches all the basic skills of mountaineering.

Bouldering is the art of making low-altitude climbs parallel to the ground. Moving horizontally along the face of a cliff only a few feet above its base, the climber confronts many of the same problems found in vertical ascents, but with a minimum of risk. This exercise is ideal for everyone. It trains the muscles, sharpens the reflexes, increases stamina, and builds confidence. But this sport is much more than just scrambling about on some rocks; it is an art with rules to learn and techniques to master.

The primary rule of bouldering is to never climb higher than you are afraid to fall. This rule sounds simple, but it must always be kept in mind. One short burst of enthusiasm is all it takes to put a climber in a dangerous position. Personally, I think six feet is a safe height if the ground below is clear, but this boundary may be drastically reduced if the cliff bottom is strewn with ankle-twisting scree. Push to your limit, but stop short of courting danger.

The second rule of climbing is to always keep three of your limbs (two arms and one leg or two legs and one arm) in solid contact with the rock while using the fourth limb to move forward. This three-point method is crucial to keeping a climber safe from falls, and the boulderer who uses it will move much farther along a cliff than one who dangles from one hand while stretching to reach the next foothold. Impress the importance of this technique on your children, and you can rest easier when they do any of the unsupervised climbing they will surely try when they are out of your sight. Besides using good sense in choosing where to climb, no other factor can guarantee the success and safety of a climber as much as the three-point technique.

An untrained mountaineer will step out on a ledge, hugging the rock and reaching high. But experienced climbers do things differently;

they are balance climbers and make efficient use of body mechanics to conserve energy and ensure their stability on the rock. Watch them and the first thing you will notice is that they are standing away from the face of the cliff, much the way a person stands away from the rungs of a ladder while climbing it. This stance may appear to be reckless, but seasoned climbers know that standing upright and away from the rock keeps their weight over their feet, increasing traction and reducing the tendency of the feet to slip. This posture is quite logical when you think about it. For if you tip the top half of your body forward, the bottom half tends to move out in reverse. This action/reaction is a prime example of Newton's third law of motion, and those who ignore such basic physics are not likely to become successful climbers.

Balance climbing also conserves energy by utilizing the large, strong muscles of the legs, rather than the weaker muscles in the arms. Throughout any climb, the hands should be used mainly to guide the body along the cliff, rather than as a main base of support. Choose handholds that are as low as possible and are fairly close together. This technique will reduce fatigue and improve balance. Remember, the legs are more important than the hands in good climbing, so do not constantly look up for handholds; instead, look down and pay attention to the placement of the feet.

Movement across the face of a cliff requires more than strength and balance; it also requires planning. Each move should be made only after the climber has spotted the next several moves that will come after it. Try to plan a series of small moves instead of one large lunge, which can throw you off balance. The need for planning while bouldering offers a good counter to impulsiveness, and while not denying anyone the opportunity to do something silly or spontaneous, it clearly demonstrates the importance of considering the consequences of one's choices and actions.

If you feel you need a "safety net" during a difficult portion of a climb, have someone "spot" you by walking below with their arms outstretched, ready to catch you or cushion your fall. This arms-out position is important because a fall can occur before the spotter can react and raise his or her arms. However, the nice thing about bouldering is that in most instances the climbers can try to do their best and simply "peel off" and drop to the ground if they get stuck or lose control of the situation.

When you find a good cliff to climb, make an effort to return to it regularly. After each visit, mark the farthest point you have moved along the cliff face. A pile of rocks or a chalk mark in a sheltered nook can indicate the outer limit of each day's best climb. Mark your progress a few times, and I guarantee that you will never walk past this special place without itching to have a go at beating your old record. In time, you will master the cliff and the climb will become easy. You will know what cracks and ledges can be depended upon to hold your weight, how the rock feels when the sun warms it, how the cliff changes color after a rainy spell. In short, you will become friendly with the mountain and a little more intimate with this great mass of rock we call Earth.

Learning
from
Lightning

Tomorrow, 8 million energy beams will strike the earth, each one five times hotter than the surface of the sun and more powerful than the atomic bomb dropped on Hiroshima. Of course, there is nothing to be concerned about; this happens all the time.

At any given moment, there are 2,000 thunderstorms passing over the surface of the planet, and these storms are generating a total of 100 lightning strikes per second. The fact that the earth is hit with approximately 1 trillion volts every day may seem awesome to most of us, but to a meteorologist it is quite routine.

A lightning bolt is actually an enormous spark arching between a positively charged area and a negatively charged one. Most often, lightning will travel between the unevenly charged areas of a thunderhead. However, 2 out of every 10 flashes are likely to strike the ground. This phenomenon usually occurs when the negative charge at the bottom of the thunderhead builds to a point that can overcome the insulation normally provided by the air. Only then can it discharge its energy into the positively charged ground below.

Because of these cloud-to-ground flashes, it is a good idea to head indoors or return to the car when the first rumbles of thunder are heard in the distance. The noise poses no danger, but where there is thunder, there is lightning; and lightning should never be taken lightly. Every year an average of 100 people in the United States are killed by lightning and another 200 or 300 are injured. The real tragedy is that almost all of these deaths and injuries could have been avoided if only the people involved had been more cautious.

The safest places to be during a thunderstorm are inside a house, away from open windows, screen doors, telephones, plumbing, and electrical appliances; or in a car (not a convertible), with the doors closed and the windows rolled up. Do not, however, seek cover under a tall tree. This is the place where the most people get hurt. If it is impossible to get to a car or solid building, seek shelter in a low area under a thick growth of brush and small trees. In an open area with little foliage, move to a low place such as a gully, ravine, or valley. Stay clear of wire fences when thunderstorms are nearby; they can carry a fatal charge up to a mile away from the point at which lightning strikes them.

If you make it to a safe haven before the storm actually hits, the lightning can tell you whether the storm is likely to pass overhead. Note the direction of the flashes. If they appear to the northwest, west, or southwest, prepare for the storm. If they appear in any other direction, you will probably be lucky and the storm will pass north or south of your position.

The color of distant lightning can also indicate if a storm is headed your way. White lightning means you are seeing the flash through the clean, dust-free air that precedes a storm. Red, orange, or yellow lightning flashes mean the air between you and the storm is laden with dust and are a sign that the storm will pass to the north or south. In general, summer storms will pass you by unless the lightning is white.

Children are usually more concerned about thunder than lightning, and some of them are quite terrified by the rumble and roar of a summer storm. Explain to them that thunder is the sound made when a bolt of lightning rapidly heats and expands the air it passes through, causing a shock wave that moves out from the lightning the same way ripples do when a pebble is tossed into water. Then tell them that thunder helps us by letting us know how far away the storm really is.

To calculate the distance between yourself and a thunderstorm, count the seconds between the time you see the flash of lightning and the time you hear the thunder (one Mississippi, two Mississippi, three Mississippi ... *bang!*). Divide the number of seconds by five and the answer is the distance to the storm in miles. This technique works because light travels at a speed that reaches our eyes almost immediately (186,000 miles per second; fast enough to get to the moon and back in 2.5 seconds), while sound travels much more slowly at about 1,000 feet per second, or almost 1 mile every 5 seconds.

During a typical storm, you will begin to hear thunder when the lightning is about 10 miles away. Thunder can be heard at greater distances if conditions are right, but you will rarely hear the sound of thunder more than 15 miles distant from the lightning bolt that produced it. At these longer distances, thunder has a lower pitch to its sound since many of its high-frequency sound waves are filtered out before they reach you. Beyond the 15-mile limit, we usually see only the flash of the lightning but are outside the range of thunder. This accounts for what is commonly known as *heat lightning*, or distant lightning without the sound of thunder.

Look for signs of lightning strikes the next time you are in the woods. The most frequently found clue is a wound several inches wide running down the trunk of a tree. If the tree has been hit recently, the wound will show the light-colored heartwood normally hidden beneath the bark. Older wounds appear as dark scars in the bark. These lightning scars can go straight down the trunk of a tree or spiral around it until they reach the ground. They are quite common, and once you have found one, you will see them during almost every future outing. Take notice of the type of trees that are hit most often. Folk wisdom and several studies all agree that oaks are hit more than other species, while beech trees are rarely struck. See if your own observations agree.

Bodysurfing

ℐ don't remember exactly when I first learned to ride waves, but I do remember that it was my father who taught me how. The surf was "small" that day, running only three or four feet high, but it looked huge to me.

My father showed me how to get into position, swim a few strokes when the right wave came, and ride it in toward the shore. I traveled only about 10 feet on my first wave before I found myself tumbling around on the bottom, my nose full of water and my swimming trunks full of sand. The ride was exhilarating, but I wasn't sure I would ever try it again. I sat out the next few waves until the newfound thrill of rocketing along with them became too strong to resist. Then I went out and caught another one. I never stopped after that, and last summer I passed on the basic skills I learned that day to my own sons.

The primary rule of bodysurfing is that to get good rides, you need to catch good waves. However, not all waves can be ridden, so it's important to learn a little about how waves form and how they break.

Waves are generated out at sea by the force of strong winds associated with storms. The energy from these winds is transferred to the water and moves through it in the form of long, unbroken waves called *swells*. As these swells near shore, the energy in them is forced upward as the sea bottom rises. This incline and the height of the swell then shape the breaking wave into one of four forms: plunging—the crest of the wave collapses into the trough, forming a tube; spilling—the crest advances as a line of foam that spills down the forward slope; collapsing—foam and turbulence form ahead of the crest on the lower half of the wave; and surging—little turbulence or foam occurs as the water surges up the beach. Only two of these forms, plunging and spilling, can give you a ride. If you find either of the other two wave forms at your beach, just figure on a day of swimming; bodysurfing is out of the question.

To catch a wave, you must go out just beyond the place where they begin to break. Your first attempts should take place in an area with a sandy bottom and in waves around three feet high. The sandy bottom is important in case you misjudge a wave and get bounced around on the bottom. The three-foot height recommendation is important because waves break when they reach water that is one and one-third times as deep (between waves) as the wave is high. Thus, you will be standing in only four feet of water while waiting for your first wave.

While waiting, keep your eyes on the waves coming toward you. When the one you want gets close, lean forward, push off from the bottom, and swim several quick strokes to get your body moving at the same speed as the wave. Now the moment you have waited for arrives: the wave does not pass beneath you, but begins to carry you forward.

At this moment, drop your head and hunch your shoulders down into the water so they are lower than the rest of your body. This position (the hardest thing for a neophyte bodysurfer to learn) will get you moving down along the forward slope of the wave. Then, keeping your body rigid, lift your head up and enjoy the ride. As someone once said, "It's the closest thing to being born."

Bodysurfing is the perfect activity for older children and young adults who are looking for some adventure and excitement. For their early rides, have them keep their hands stretched out in front to prevent any mishaps that might occur should one of them suddenly "discover" the bottom. This is most likely to happen if he or she gets caught in the falling tubular crest of a plunging wave. Surfers call it "going over the falls," and it usually results from a late start. Stay with the smaller waves until you learn more advanced techniques from other bodysurfers. Soon you will all be able to dip one shoulder into the wave and ride across its face rather than straight in to shore. However, one must learn to walk before one can learn to run, and the techniques you have just read are only the first step. But who knows where these early steps will lead? Perhaps one day you or the children you teach will ride the "ultimate" surf that rolls in at Makapuu, Hawaii—a place where the waves and their riders can grow to become legends.

Snowfall

Grown-ups are always willing to see the worst in falling snow. When they look at this cascade of featherlight crystals, they imagine only slippery roads, snow-covered sidewalks, and the tracks of wet boots on clean floors.

This cynicism is born of busy schedules, and it causes adults to stay indoors during snowstorms and miss the chance to introduce children to some of winter's most amazing sights.

The most widely enjoyed snowstorm activity is simply observing individual snowflakes as they land on clothing. To do this, stand outside long enough for the surface of your clothing to cool down, and stick out your arm. Soon falling snowflakes will land on your sleeve, and if the fabric is cold enough, the snowflakes will remain there undamaged.

Look closely at the tiny crystals resting on your sleeve. If the individual snowflakes are star-shaped (the type usually found when the temperature is around 32°F), you are in luck, and your children are about to get a lesson on how infinite variety can be developed from a single theme.

Have the children look closely at the starlike snowflakes, and ask them to tell you what each one has in common with all the others. In no time at all, one of them will notice that each one of the "stars" has six arms. This is the answer you are looking for—and, save for a few snowflakes that have lost one or more of their arms during their descent, this answer is quite accurate. But the real marvel of snowflakes is what comes next.

Tell the children that although billions of these six-armed stars will fall on every acre of land during a heavy snow, they will never find two of them that are exactly the same. This fact always seems to be too much for them to believe, and they will soon become engrossed in studying the snowflakes on their clothing, looking for the identical twins they will never find.

When they finally concede that every snowflake is unique in design, tell them about the other things in their world that are infinite variations on a single theme: how all numbers can be written with only 10 digits (0-9); how only 108 chemical elements make up everything on our planet; how millions of people live on earth—all human beings, yet each different from every other. There are countless examples, all of which will introduce children to a new way of understanding the world around them—the way of seeing unity in diversity.

To see snowflakes at their best, try viewing them as they fall onto a piece of black velvet. Against this dark background, every facet is highlighted and looks as if it were made of diamond. The fact that jewelers use this very same material to show off their finest gems is no accident.

A lesser-known way to enjoy a snowstorm is to look at large snow-flakes as they fall from the sky. Bring your children out into an open field, a lawn, or any place where you can see only the sky when you look straight up. Then, keeping your head up, focus your eyes on the falling snow. At first it will look as if you are peering into a sky full of falling feathers, but as you continue to stare upward, a change will come about. Suddenly, you will feel as if you are moving upward through the snow and not as if the snow is moving down toward you. It feels as if you are traveling through space with your feet on the ground.

This illusion works because we see movement by relating moving objects to the things they approach or pass by. When we only see the moving object itself, we have difficulty telling whether the object is moving toward us or whether we are moving toward it. For this reason, you must see only snow and sky when you try this activity. If a branch of a tree, a rooftop, or anything else is in view, your eyes will not be tricked.

If you cannot find an open place, try cupping your hands around your eyes to block out everything but a small patch of sky. This method lacks the panoramic quality of staring up at the open sky, but it works quite well. Try this activity next time you're out in a snowstorm and it will forever change the way you look at falling snow.

The Quinzhee

Usually, when someone mentions building with snow, the Eskimo igloo comes to mind. But an igloo is built of cut and shaped snow blocks arranged in a rising spiral that angles in toward the center, and this shelter is not easy to construct.

In fact, an expert may take several hours to build an igloo, while a novice could work all day and still not get it right. However, there is another snow shelter that is easy to build. It is the *quinzhee* (KWIN-zee)—a temporary shelter used by the native peoples of the northern United States and Canada.

A quinzhee is actually a large pile of snow that has been hollowed out on the inside. Unlike igloos, these structures do not have to be built with any special type of snow, but they do require a large amount of whatever type is available. So the first thing you should do after deciding to build one is find a large, open space where the snow is undisturbed.

When you have found a suitable site, get a snow shovel and start piling up snow. A quinzhee that will comfortably shelter 3 adults can be made from a snow pile 6 feet high and 15 feet wide, but if you are making a playhouse for the kids, reduce the size of the pile to 6 feet high by 9 or 10 feet wide. It all depends on your level of ambition and the number of helpers you have.

Once you have piled the snow, take a rest. The snow must set for several hours before you can work on it. During this period, the weight and temperature of the pile cause the snow to recrystallize and harden. On a cold day, one or two hours should be enough time, but if you can leave the pile overnight, that's even better.

After the snow has set, trade your snow shovel for a short-handled spade or entrenching tool and tunnel into the pile at ground level, keeping the entrance just large enough for one person to crawl through. When this initial tunnel is about three feet long, begin to scoop out the snow overhead and to the sides, leaving the bottom, supporting layer until last. Toss the excavated snow out of the entrance hole, and when you see the section of wall you are working on become notice-ably lighter, stop work there and move to another spot.

By removing snow until the outside light begins to filter through, you will make the interior of the quinzhee as large as it can be while allowing the walls to remain structurally sound. When you have fin-ished hollowing out the interior, poke a small hole in the roof for ven-tilation, close the entrance with a block of snow or an extra jacket, and you have finished.

Sit inside the dome-shaped room you have just created and notice how much warmer and quieter it is inside. Explain to anyone with you that while they are inside the quinzhee, they are in the same *subnivian* (under the snow) environment that deer mice and meadow voles inhabit all winter. It is interesting to imagine what it might be like to live like this.

If your quinzhee is in the backyard or some other easily accessible place, take some children to it for a nighttime storytelling. Dress warmly, bring a ground cloth to sit on, a candle for light, and a ripping-good tale to tell the kids. You are about to take the children on a journey far into the human past, to a time when wondrous stories were told around the family fire.

Be sure to go inside the quinzhee before the children and light the candle. This preparation allows the children to experience the full contrast of moving from the darkness of the winter night to the bright and cozy atmosphere inside the quinzhee. Once inside, they will surely marvel at the way the candlelight glistens on every ridge and facet in the snow walls; they will feel as if they are inside a diamond.

When everyone is inside, block off the entrance and give them some time to settle down. Soon the heat from your bodies will warm up the interior, and a sense of comradeship will begin to pervade the group. Now is the time to begin your tale.

Although almost any story will be wonderful when you tell it in a candlelit quinzhee, those stories that take place in the frozen North capture the mood set by the snowy walls and the cold weather. My favorite tale for a windy winter night is "The Cremation of Sam McGee" by Robert W. Service. If you don't know a good story, ask the children's librarian at the local library to recommend some. They will know how to find the right story for this special occasion.

If possible, build the quinzhee in a shady area or on the north side of your house. By doing this, you will protect the snow walls from the sun, and, in colder areas, the structure will remain intact for quite some time. There is one other precaution to be taken if want your quinzhee to last. Be sure to tell the neighborhood children that there is more to that large pile of snow in the yard than meets the eye. The first time I built one, a local teenager took a running start and tried to scale my snow pile on the side away from the entrance hole. She couldn't have known what she was getting into, and, almost instantly, the roof caved in and she found herself up to her waist in the snow she had assumed was solid. That was the end of that quinzhee, for the snow walls cannot be repaired once they have been breached. The incident was unfortunate, but there have been other snows and I've built other quinzhees—all in the most remote corners of my yard.

Falling Waters

Waterfalls have a magnetic quality that seems to attract human beings. No one has ever defined this attraction. But you cannot walk past one of these columns of falling water without stopping in admiration.

The major attraction of waterfalls may be the mesmerizing effect they have on us. When we first view them, we are exhilarated, but after this initial impression has passed, they become somehow soothing and conducive to daydreams. The sound of the water crashing into the pool below is an attraction, as is the moist breeze created by the cascading water. One theory states that people are drawn to waterfalls because the air there is charged with negative ions that give them a feeling of well-being. But whatever the reason, there is one thing I know for sure: I have never found a waterfall without a well-worn path leading to it.

Waterfalls are usually quite young in geological terms and are formed at the point where a stream or river passes from a layer of hard rock to a layer of softer rock. At this point, the sand and gravel carried by the current begin to erode the softer rock faster than the harder rock, and an irregularity develops in the streambed that may later turn into a waterfall. Look at the rock wall behind a waterfall and you will often find that it is composed of two differently colored layers of rock. The bottom layer is the softer rock that was cut away to form the falls.

This unequal rate of erosion is responsible for the creation of 90 percent of all waterfalls. However, if you ask people how waterfalls are formed, most of them will tell you a story about streams that were traveling toward the sea when they happened upon the cliffs over which they now flow. This story is nice, but it is rarely true. Waterfalls are evidence of the power water can exert in shaping the land; they are not chance happenings.

When you are standing at the base of a waterfall, you can enjoy it from a different perspective—one drop at a time. Throw your head back, look up, and find a place (usually off to the side of the main flow) where the water is steadily dripping. Now, focus your eyes on this place and pick out an individual drop as it begins its descent. Keep your eyes focused on the drop, but don't follow it down with your eyes alone. Instead, roll your head forward and down as the drop falls. By watching in this manner, you will be able to see the shape and movement of the single drop as it falls through the air.

If you follow the drop with your eyes alone, all you will see is a streak. But if you roll your head downward as the drop descends, it will look like a clear, pulsating globe moving slowly through the air. This globe shape often surprises people, most of whom believe that all drops of water are teardrop-shaped and streamlined. It is a lesson in how direct experience should be used to check popular beliefs and can demonstrate the value of thinking for oneself.

When the light is right and the weather is mild, you may have a hard time persuading people to continue on with the hike. Often they will cease drop watching only after they have developed a crick in their necks from so much head rolling. But before you leave, you can enjoy one more activity while watching drops of water plummet from a waterfall—an activity that will impress your friends with your knowledge of mathematics and science.

Using the head-rolling technique described above, focus your attention on a drop of water as it begins its descent, and count the number of seconds it takes for that drop to hit the bottom (one Mississippi, two Mississippi, three Mississippi, *splash*). Multiply the number of seconds by itself, and multiply the answer by 16. What does all of this multiplication tell you? Amazingly, the answer is the height of the waterfall in feet.

This formula (seconds^2 x 16 = feet fallen) works because all free-falling objects accelerate at the same speed. If you are at the top of a waterfall cliff or any other elevated site and want to know how far it is to the bottom, drop a pebble over the side and start counting the seconds. This technique always works and is quite accurate. It is nothing magical, only applied physics.

Images
on the
Moon

The full moon has always fascinated people who have considered it a god, a demon, good luck, bad luck, the ripener of crops, the cause of madness, and so many other things that the number alone is a fitting tribute to the fertility of human imagination.

For centuries, the moon was an important part of the way people experienced the night; but with the advent of electricity, our nighttime habits changed, and we began to spend our evenings indoors. Soon we stopped looking at the moon, and today we can safely assume that, on any given night, most people will not know what phase the moon is in—a fact that sadly proves how much modern living has dulled our awareness of nature.

The hardest of moons to ignore are the giant, round ones we sometimes see as they are rising in the east. At one time or another, everyone has marveled at one of these, for they have a beautiful, eerie quality that demands our attention. But what most people don't know is that they can "shrink" these huge moons back down to normal size.

The gigantic proportions of a full moon near the horizon is an illusion, and—as with all illusions—this one can be shattered if you know the right technique. In this case, all you need to do is hold your hand so it blocks out the horizon below the moon. As soon as you do this, the moon showing above your hand reverts to the size you normally expect it to be. No one knows exactly why this optical shift happens, but in A.D. 150, Ptolemy put forth a theory that is seemingly verified by this hand-blocking technique. His theory states that the moon appears larger when it is low in the sky because we are seeing it in comparison to trees, buildings, mountains, and other objects whose size we know. Our eyes use these objects as frames of reference, and the moon seems immense in relation to them.

As the full moon climbs into the night sky, it naturally shrinks down to normal size because we have nothing with which to compare it in the empty void of space. But even at its zenith, this shining orb so dominates the night that we can easily understand why it has inspired so many myths and customs.

The patterns on the face of the full moon have also inspired their own legends and tales. Ask your friends to tell you what pictures they see when they look at the spots on the moon's surface. For Americans, the most familiar lunar image is the face of the man in the moon. With his two large, round eyes and a round, open mouth, he is what most of us see when we indulge in a bit of moon gazing. But although this picture may be familiar, it is only a product of imaginations that have been molded by the cultural traditions that were passed on to us.

People in other countries see different images in the lunar disk. For example, millions of people in India see a rabbit when they look at the moon. And, as is true for most moon pictures, they have a story to go along with it—a good story to tell around a campfire or during an evening walk.

The story begins with a ragged, starving beggar wandering through a forest. As he traveled beneath the tall, dark trees, he met a fox, a monkey, and a rabbit. After telling the animals that he had not eaten for many, many days, the beggar asked the animals to get him some food. The animals took pity on the poor man and vowed to find something for him to eat. Soon they were all searching the entire region for food.

Fox returned with a bowl of milk, and Monkey brought a handful of mangoes. But Rabbit returned empty-handed. "I have failed to find any food for you," Rabbit confessed to the beggar. "But since you will soon die if you do not eat, build a fire, roast me, and eat me for dinner."

The beggar moaned that he was truly starving, and started to build the fire. As the flames leaped higher, Rabbit ran across the ground and jumped right into them. Fox and Monkey turned their heads, for they could not bear to see what was happening to their friend. But before Rabbit's furry feet even touched the hot coals of the fire, the beggar grabbed him by his long ears, pulled him to safety, and set him down on the cool ground.

"What happened?" Rabbit wondered. And as he sat there shivering with fear, he saw the beggar change into the great god Indra. "Fox and Monkey have brought me food," said Indra. "But you, Rabbit, would have given your own life to feed me. As a reward, I will carry you up to the moon where you will live forever in perfect happiness." And that is why, even today, many people of India can see the rabbit in the face of the full moon.

The Japanese also see a rabbit in the moon, whereas the Dutch see a cabbage thief and his cabbages. If you look long enough, you may find the young woman, grandmother, toad, mouse, bear, lion, or fox that the people of other cultures have seen there. Have your friends hunt for these shapes. It is an enjoyable activity that can be done while lying on a blanket in the backyard or while taking an evening walk. You should all memorize one that you find to be especially appealing. That way, no matter where you go, the moon will always remain a familiar face and retrieve fond memories.

A Star to Guide You

In America, the star pattern we call the Big Dipper got its name from early European settlers, who thought these seven stars looked like the long-handled ladles they used to scoop water from a bucket. However, not everyone looked at these stars in this way.

The English saw this group of stars as a plow, the Poles named it "the wagon," and Pacific Islanders perceived it as a rat. In fact, the Big Dipper did not become a constellation in its own right because the Romans declared that these stars were only a part of Ursa Major, the Great Bear. Today's astronomers call the Big Dipper an *asterism,* which is a star pattern that does not belong to one of the 88 groups of stars officially recognized as constellations. Yet, even though this star group may lack official recognition, it is undeniably the most widely known pattern of stars in the northern night sky.

To find the Big Dipper, stand facing north and search the sky for the seven stars forming its outline. There will be four stars in the handle, and the remaining three outline the bowl. This search should be easy, for all the stars are quite bright; and, in contrast to the official constellations, the Big Dipper actually looks like the thing for which it was named.

Another reason it is easy to identify this star group is that, unlike most star patterns, you can see the Big Dipper every night of the year throughout much of the Northern Hemisphere. You may be in Pittsburgh or Paris, but if the sky is clear and your location is above 40 degrees north latitude, every star in the Big Dipper will be visible tonight. The reason for this constant presence is that the Big Dipper is located above the northern polar region of our planet, and this segment of the sky is never blocked from view as the earth turns. Stars in this position, called *circumpolar stars,* never set below the horizon, but appear to move in a circle around the star we call Polaris—the North Star.

For centuries, before the invention of the compass, those who traveled at night used the North Star to determine direction. The Native Americans as well as the Vikings used this star as a guide; and Columbus steered by it on his journeys to the New World. They all found this particular star useful for navigation because it never moves from a position located almost directly over the North Pole. When you look straight at it, you are facing north, with east to the right, west to the left, and your back to the south. Armed with this information and a general idea of the direction you should travel, you will never be lost.

To locate Polaris, which is a star of the second magnitude and not very prominent, you must first find the Big Dipper. Once you have found it, draw an imaginary line between the two stars at the end of the bowl opposite the handle, and extend this line upward about five times until it leads you close to a fairly bright star. This star is Polaris. The two stars that guided you—Merak and Dubhe—are so famous for this function that they are known as the *pointers*, and by using them, you can always orient yourself on a clear night. Younger children, many of whom may have some fears about getting lost, frequently find this technique to be very reassuring. They gain a feeling of competence and a sense of security.

At first glance, there appears to be seven stars in the Big Dipper. But look closely at the middle star in the handle. If the night is clear and dark, and your eyesight is average, you will be able to pick out a tiny star immediately adjacent to the middle star. The larger star is named Mizar, and the smaller one is called Alcor. Before the invention of eye charts, these stars were used to test people's vision. If a person could see both stars on a clear night, his or her vision was assumed to be normal. Today, there are far more accurate methods of measuring eyesight, but if one of your companions cannot see the smaller star that everyone else has in sight, it may be wise for her or him to see an optometrist.

Because Mizar is a second-magnitude star while Alcor is only about one-quarter as bright, this pair of stars has been given many different names. The Arabs called them "The Horse and the Rider," and some Native American tribes named them "The Little Papoose on the Big Squaw's Back." My favorite description of these two stars is given by the Iroquois. They say that the three bright stars in the handle of the Big Dipper are hunters, and that the bowl is a bear the hunters are pursuing. It was said that the hunters must be sure they will make the kill, because the middle one carries a pot to cook the bear in.

If you are outside during the day and want to get your bearings, there is another star that can act as a guide—that very special one we call the sun. This star, which gives warmth and light to our planet, rises in the eastern part of the sky and sets in the western part every day of the year. But on two days each year, the sunrise is due east and the sunset is due west. These two days are usually March 21 and September 21, the dates of the equinoxes. After the spring equinox, the sun will rise to the north of east at sunrise and will go down north of west at sunset. It will do just the opposite after the autumnal equinox and rise and set to the south of east and west. But at all times it can give you a good general idea of which way is which.

If you need to get your bearings during the middle of the day, you can use your wristwatch. To do this, first point the hour hand of your watch directly toward the sun (remembering to subtract an hour if the watch is set for daylight savings time) by holding a small twig or matchstick upright against the edge of the watch and lining the hour hand up with the shadow. Once this is done, find the number that is halfway (going the shortest way) between the hour hand and the number 12, and draw an imaginary line from that number to the center of the watch. This line is running from north to south.

Although I have often taken people out in the backyard to show them how to navigate by the stars or by using a wristwatch, nothing can compare with teaching children about the Big Dipper while lying around in sleeping bags after the campfire has died down. In an atmosphere such as this, they not only learn to read the stars, they also develop an appreciation for the consistency, poetry, and wonderful vastness of the night sky.

Skipping Stones, Sand Castles, & Memories in Clay

Flowing water is the great leveler of the earth's surface. Moving ever downward, it abrades the rocky crust of the planet and, bit by bit, wears down high mountains to fill up deep valleys. Geologists call this process *erosion,* and it makes possible several outdoor activities that would otherwise be nonexistent.

As water moves over stones, it smoothes their rough surfaces and rounds their edges until they become the flat, pancake-shaped rocks so common along the shores of rivers and streams. Technically speaking, this smooth, flat, rounded shape forms because it offers the least resistance to the onrushing water, but if you ask me, these rocks were ground down for just one purpose: to create skipping stones.

Also known as dapping, ge-plunking, and ducks and drakes, the ancient art of skipping stones requires only quiet water, a good arm, and the smooth stones mentioned above. Look for stones that are two to three inches in diameter and have the flattest sides and roundest edges. When you spot one, pick it up. If it feels a little heavy for its size, you have a prime skipping stone; one you should save for the "let's-see-who-can-skip-one-the-farthest" tournaments that often arise whenever two or more people decide to ricochet rocks across the water.

When you are ready to skip your stone, wrap your index finger around its back edge and hold it in place with your thumb. Then, holding the stone firmly in this position, draw back your arm, and using a sidearm pitch, throw the stone as low and even with the water's surface as possible. If the stone is traveling nearly parallel to the water and has its forward edge slightly raised when it makes contact, it will plane across the water in a series of long skips (called *plinkers*) followed by a rapid series of short skips (called *pittypats*). The force of the throw should be entirely forward. If you throw the stone with any downward force, it will either dive directly beneath the water or make one grand leap into the air, only to fall back and sink to the bottom.

You can skip stones anywhere there is relatively calm water. Obviously, a glassy lake or pond is the ideal location, but I have bounced smooth stones off the rounded crests of ocean waves rolling in beyond the surf line. As long as the surface is not choppy, you can get at least a few skips on almost any reasonably sized body of water. Whenever you feel ready for some big-time stone skipping, try topping the world record. At present, 38 skips (plinkers plus pittypats) holds the title, but anything over 20 hops is enough to make you a top-notch competitor.

As the flowing water that shaped skipping stones continues to wear down quartz, feldspar, mica, and a number of other minerals, it forms the small-particle soil commonly known as *sand*. People have used sand to make glass, to blast graffiti from walls, and, when mixed with cement, to build most of the world's cities. But to the young at heart, sand is for play, and the apex of this play is the construction of sand castles.

If you doubt the appeal of sand castling, watch children next time you are on the beach. Almost without exception, sometime during the day, every kid with a bucket is going to fill it up, pack it down, and flip it over in the hope of making a perfectly formed tower of sand. The children may build mounds, dikes, channels, pits, and walls, but always, somewhere near the center, they will build a sand castle.

The creation of most sand castles requires a container of some sort to mold the sand, but one type of castle can be constructed without any tools except the hands of the builder. Most people call them *drip sand castles,* and if you know how to make one, you will have a chance to show off and be an inspiration to every kid on the beach.

Before you try to build a drip sand castle, you should test the sand and determine if it will hold together through the dripping process. To do this, pick up a handful of dry sand, squeeze it, and then open your hand, letting the sand drop to the ground. If your hand is left well covered with sand, the sand grains are fine enough for good sand castling.

When the sand on the beach is good for building, move down close to the water and dig a shallow hole. The sand at this construction site should be so wet that the hole you dig immediately becomes a puddle, for only supersaturated sand can be used to create a drip sand castle of truly noble proportions. When you have found the proper spot, settle in and begin to mix up the sand and water at the bottom of the hole, taking care to remove any pebbles, shells, or other foreign matter.

After the sand has been cleaned, reach down into the bottom of the hole and scoop up a handful. Then, closing your hand into a loose fist, tip it up and let the sand slowly run through the small circle formed by your little finger and palm. If the sand has the right consistency, it will flow in a thin and steady stream. Direct this stream over one spot, and, little by little, a spire will begin to grow up from the ground as the sand piles up on top of itself.

The dripping sand will set and begin to dry almost as soon as it hits the ground. After a few tries, you should be able to regulate the stream of flowing sand so the piles you make grow quite high before they collapse. With practice and the right sand, you can build a drip sand castle several feet high and of an elfin delicacy that other sand castles can never match. Don't worry if you can't devote much time to mastering this technique; even with mediocre sand, you can build a drip sand castle over one foot tall on the first try. Besides, these structures are so much fun to make that everyone around will want to work on their own sand castles long before yours ever gets too tall.

Although drip sand castles may look unnatural and much like futuristic towers from some other world, they are really quite similar to stalagmites—those eerie columns growing up from the floors of caves. Stalagmites form when water, which has been continuously dripping onto the same spot of a cave floor, evaporates and leaves behind the minerals it had dissolved. But unlike stalagmites, which grow stronger as the water evaporates, sand castles disintegrate as they dry. This happens because the sand castle is held together by the tension of the water surrounding the grains of sand and not by the grains themselves. When the water evaporates, the individual grains of sand fall prey to gravity and drop back to the beach. All is the same as it was before you arrived.

When water grinds rock down to particles even smaller in size than sand, it eventually forms the soil we know as *clay*. Like the terms *pebbles*, *sand*, and *silt*, clay refers only to the size of the particles in a given soil and not to their chemical composition. Clay is composed mostly of particles smaller than two microns (.00008 inches) and has an undeniable appeal to those who enjoy its cool, slippery texture and its malleable qualities.

When you are on an outing, try to find a deposit of clay. This search is usually not very difficult, since clay is one of the most abundant materials on the face of the earth. Look along the banks of rivers and streams, road cuts, or building sites where the topsoil has been removed. Clay can be gray, brown, beige, red, or almost any other earthen color, but a consistent coloration and smooth texture will be the signs that your search has been successful.

To determine if your discovery is workable clay and worth playing with, try the following tests. First, pick up a small handful of the soil you are analyzing, wet it down if it is dry, and then rub a pinch of it between your fingers. The sample should feel smoother and stickier than other soils. Next, roll the soil into a small ball between the palms of your hands and then roll this ball out into a long, pencil-thin strand. If the clay is usable, this strand will show few cracks when you coil it around one of your fingers.

Kneading is the first step in preparing clay, so begin by squeezing the clay, folding it over, and squeezing it again. Pick out any impurities and crumble the dry lumps of clay until the whole thing has a consistency something like very thick whipped cream. This kneading process is the same as the one performed with bread dough, but the purpose is exactly the opposite. When making bread, the object is to trap air bubbles in the dough so the bread will rise. When preparing clay, the goal is to remove the air bubbles because they will form weak spots in the clay when it dries.

Once you have finished kneading the clay, its possible uses are almost limitless. For thousands of years, people have made cups, pots, beads, flutes, statues, and numerous other items from this material. Yet of all the ancient clay objects found in museums today, the artifacts that most capture the imagination are the clay tablets from Mesopotamia, the ones covered with the mysterious script we call *cuneiform*. We may not be able to read what is written on these clay tablets, but we can certainly appreciate how these hard bricks have carried the thoughts of some ancient person across time and preserved them for posterity. The longevity of these clay messages demonstrates a way for children to leave a record of their visit without carving their initials into a tree or spray painting a rock. By using clay, they can create a memorial to themselves without defacing the environment.

To construct the personal artifact commemorating their visit, prepare the clay as described, and pat it down into thick, flat disks of any size that seems appropriate. Next, have the children print their initials, compose messages, or make pictures in the soft clay. Encourage everyone to use their imagination. They can make prints by pressing different objects into the soft surface of the clay, or they can make personal fossils by leaving an impression of their thumbs and fingers.

My favorite clay project is to make a thumbprint and draw a face inside of it. This activity is especially satisfying, because when I return at some future date, my thumb will be the only one that fits perfectly into the imprint, just as only Cinderella's foot could fit into the glass slipper. This activity is also wonderful for growing children who, upon reclaiming their disks, find a thumbprint of the smaller child they once were—a fossil-like record of their recent past.

When the children have finished their handiwork, set the clay disks out in the sun until they are dry and hard. Even on a very hot day, this setting process will take over an hour, so take the kids off to do something else for a while. When the clay has hardened, have the children hide their disks in places that offer protection from the rain and snow. Rock crevices, tree holes, or the bases of trunks of thick evergreens are all good locations. Theoretically, these mementos will last indefinitely if they are undisturbed and protected from the elements, and children cherish the idea of having something that is uniquely theirs securely hidden in some secret spot deep in the woods.

The Measure of All Things

Several years ago, I took my sons hiking in the woods where I had spent most of my free time as a child. We trudged through low swamp and brush for about an hour, and finally we came to a rise in the land where some early settler had once lived.

Not much was left of this old homestead. Only a few crumbling walls and a leaf-filled cellar hole marked the spot where the house once stood. But a pair of giant Norway spruces grew along the path to what once was the front door, and these were a sight to behold. The old pioneer's landscaping had long outlived his architecture.

The two trees dominated the hilltop we stood on, and it wasn't long before one of the boys asked, "How tall do you think those trees are?" It was the moment I had waited for. I now had my chance to show off some basic trigonometry while appearing to possess the wisdom of the ancients. I answered, "I can measure these trees with a twig." Suddenly, all eyes were upon me.

This little trick of measuring a tree with a stick is called the *thumb jump*. It requires no special skills; in fact, as long as you know the height of the person you are with, you can easily accomplish this feat.

Have your companion stand up against the tree you want to measure while you find a stick. Next, step back far enough so you can easily see the top and bottom of the object to be measured and hold the stick upright at arm's length. Sight over the top of the stick and line it up with the top of your friend's head. Then, holding the stick steady, move your thumb down the side of the stick until it lines up with that person's feet. Now comes the thumb jumping. Holding your thumb snug against the stick, move your arm upward until your thumb is lined up with the head of the person standing against the tree. Note the spot where the top of the stick now stops on the trunk of the tree and "jump" your thumb up to that place. Continue jumping your thumb until you reach the top of the tree you are measuring, and then multiply the number of times you jumped the stick up the tree by the height of your companion. The result is the height of the tree.

On the day I measured those Norway spruces, my son was five feet tall. Since I had to jump my thumb 18 times his height to reach the tops of the trees, I knew that these magnificent specimens stood 90 feet tall. The boys quickly learned this technique, and by the end of the day, there wasn't an upright item in the woods that they hadn't measured.

The thumb jump can be used on anything vertical, not just trees. I've used it to measure flagpoles, cliffs, and skyscrapers. However, children are often more interested in how many times larger the object is than themselves. To a four-foot child, the idea of stacking 20 of herself is more impressive than an abstract measure of height.

The width of a stream is another natural feature worth knowing how to measure—especially if it is one you are considering jumping across. How can you tell if you can make the leap from one bank to the other? Simple. Stand facing the stream and look at the spot where you want to land on the far bank. Then, put your chin down to your chest and raise your hand up so its inside edge covers both eyebrows in something like a salute. Next, rotate the hand you have on your eyebrows downward until its lower edge lines up with the spot across the stream. Now, keeping your hand and head in the same position, rotate your body and look for something on your shore that lines up with the lower edge of your hand. The distance between that object and yourself is equal to the width of the stream. If you can leap that far, you have a good chance of making it across the stream without getting wet. This technique is quite accurate and will help keep your socks dry.

Later in the day, when the sun is getting low, you will want to know how long you have until sunset. If you have ever fumbled and stumbled your way back to camp in the dark, you know what I mean.

Generations of sailors have used the following technique, but you can adapt it to any situation where you can get a clear view of the sun above the horizon. Hold your arm out straight with the hand turned in and the palm facing you. Keeping the fingers extended and the thumb tucked in, position your hand so it fits between the horizon and the bottom of the sun. If you can fit four extended fingers between the sun and the horizon, there is one hour remaining until sunset. If only two fingers fit, you have roughly 30 minutes. Each finger equals about 15 minutes, and each hand about one hour. With a little practice, you can predict quite precisely the time the sun will dip below the horizon.

Of course, not all hands are the same size, and the width of a child's hand may be only half the size of an adult's—a fact that can seriously alter the accuracy of this technique. Fortunately, adjusting this activity for children is quite simple. First, have each child hold one arm straight out with the hand turned in as described above. Next, have them line up the bottom edge of the outstretched hand with the horizon. When the hand is in position, have them alternately place one hand on top of the other until one of their hands is directly overhead. Divide the number of hands it takes to do this into 90 (the number of degrees between the horizon and the zenith) and multiply by 4 (the number of minutes equal to one degree of an arc). The result of all this arithmetic is the number of minutes each hand equals. The following chart gives you the time equivalents for several different hand widths.

Number of Hands between Horizon and Zenith	Time Each Hand Equals (in minutes)
6	60
7	51
8	45
9	40
10	36
11	33
12	30

With this field measure, you can always be sure to get back before dark. However, if you take your siting in a field or clearing and have to travel through a wooded area on the way home, remember that beneath the canopy of the trees, darkness arrives about 20 minutes earlier on a clear day and up to an hour earlier if the sky is overcast. Plan for the end of the day as well as you would for its beginning, and things are bound to work out fine.

Index

136